TOP-DOWN COLORWORK KNIT

Sweaters and Accessories

STACKPOLE BOOKS

An imprint of Globe Pequot, the trade division of The Rowman & Littlefield Publishing Group, Inc.
4501 Forbes Blvd., Ste. 200
Lanham, MD 20706
www.rowman.com

Distributed by NATIONAL BOOK NETWORK
800-462-6420

© 2020 Edition Michael Fischer GmbH, www.emf-verlag.de
This edition of ISLANDPULLOVER STRICKEN first published in Germany by Edition Michael Fischer GmbH in 2020 is published by arrangement with Silke Bruenink Agency, Munich, Germany.

Design: © 2020 Edition Michael Fischer, from the book "Islandpullover stricken" ("Knitting Icelandic sweaters")
© 2020 Edition Michael Fischer GmbH, Donnersbergstr. 7, 86859 Igling, Germany
Cover design, layout, typesetting: Meritt Hettwer
Product management: Anja Sommerfeld
Photographs: © Corinna Brix, München, Germany, except pg. 19: @ Ines Grabner, Berlin, Germany; pg. 142: © Wenke Müller
Editing: Regina Sidabras, Berlin, Germany
Image processing: Sophia Lasson
Translation: Katharina Sokiran

We have made every effort to ensure the accuracy and completeness of these instructions. We cannot, however, be responsible for human error, typographical mistakes, or variations in individual work.

British Library Cataloguing in Publication Information available

Library of Congress Cataloging-in-Publication Data
Names: Müller, Wenke, author.
Title: Top-down colorwork knit sweaters and accessories : 25 patterns for women and men / Wenke Müller ; translation: Katharina Sokiran.
Other titles: Islandpullover. English
Description: First edition. | Guilford, Connecticut : Stackpole Books, [2021] | Translation of: Islandpullover : skandinavische Top-down-Modelle mit kuschligen Accessoires stricken. | Summary: "A collection of 25 patterns for sweaters and accessories in Scandinavian style, including 3 men's sweaters. An introductory section on sweater knitting techniques for working in the round, top-down, and with two colors of yarn"— Provided by publisher.
Identifiers: LCCN 2021004747 (print) | LCCN 2021004748 (ebook) | ISBN 9780811769921 (cloth ; alk. paper) | ISBN 9780811769938 (electronic)
Subjects: LCSH: Knitting—Patterns. | Sweaters.
Classification: LCC TT825 .M785513 2021 (print) | LCC TT825 (ebook) | DDC 746.43/2041—dc23
LC record available at https://lccn.loc.gov/2021004747
LC ebook record available at https://lccn.loc.gov/2021004748

First Edition

WENKE MÜLLER

TOP-DOWN COLORWORK KNIT

Sweaters and Accessories

25 PATTERNS *for* WOMEN AND MEN

STACKPOLE BOOKS

Guilford, Connecticut

CONTENTS

MATCHING ACCESSORIES   100

PREFACE

Traditionally knitted from coarse sheep's wool, colorful circular yoke sweaters kept the inhabitants of Iceland toasty warm in the rugged environment. The stranded colorwork pattern extended over neck and shoulders and was often partially repeated above the cuffs. Nowadays, Scandinavian-style sweaters have conquered even our more temperate climates. Worked in more lightweight yarns, the designs from this book are even suitable for office wear. Sweaters can feature a more complicated stranded colorwork pattern or just sport textured or striped patterns—which makes them as versatile and diverse as their wearers. Depending on personal preferences and colors used, the garments can be worn by men as well as women.

All designs have in common that they are knitted from the top down to the bottom. This allows for working in the round, always on the right side of the fabric, and the garment-in-progess can be easily tried on for fittings (for instance, to determine the perfect sleeve length). Also, many knitters have learned to appreciate that with this construction method, there are no more annoying seams—just weave in ends and put on your new sweater! This attribute has firmly established top-down knitting as a favorite method in today's knitting circles.

To complete your stylish outfits, I have also developed an array of pretty, matching accessories to complement the garments.

I wish you much joy when knitting and showing off your "treasures"—you can be sure of receiving admiring glances!

Yours truly,

Wenke Müller

Basics

KNITTING TOP-DOWN SWEATERS WITH CIRCULAR YOKE

The sweaters in this book are worked seamlessly from the top down in the round in one piece.

WHY FROM THE TOP DOWN?

The advantage of it is, in my opinion, that the garment can be tried on and adjusted if needed while knitting. Before trying on, don't forget to transfer the live stitches to long cords or a long piece of sturdy, tear-resistant thread.

Knitting in the round is very handy, especially for stranded colorwork, since only knit stitches are worked, and yarns are crossed in back of work. This allows for even tension of the working yarn, which in turn results in a more even stitch definition. It's also much more convenient, since the working yarns in different colors can be held in one hand at the same time (see page 17, "holding the working yarn").

FIT OPTIONS AND SIZE

My circular yoke pullovers are typically unisex garments, which can be worn by women as well as men. In order to be able to offer different options for fit and size, I have decided on three different ease options called Fits, which are related to the average chest circumference measurement according to the size worked.

Slim Fit: approx. 2.4 in. (6 cm) of positive ease added to the chest circumference measurement of the wearer.

Regular Fit: approx. 5.5 in. (14 cm) of positive ease added to the chest circumference measurement of the wearer.

Loose Fit: approx. 7.2 in. (18 cm) of positive ease added to the chest circumference measurement of the wearer.

IMPORTANT: These are average positive ease amounts. Actual ease may vary, depending on the design. Exact numbers for each pattern's specific measurements and ease amounts can be found in the "size" section.

BODY MEASUREMENTS (UNISEX)				
Sizes	S	M	L	XL
Chest circumference range	32.3–36.2 in. (82–92 cm)	36.6–40.6 in. (93–103 cm)	41–44.1 in. (104–112 cm)	44.5–48 in. (113–122 cm)
Chest circumference average	34.3 in. (87 cm)	38.6 in. (98 cm)	42.5 in. (108 cm)	46.3 in. (117.5 cm)

HOW TO KNIT

Work always starts with the neckband (or the turtleneck collar for Steinunn). Before beginning the actual yoke, most of the time, a few short rows are worked, which results in the back neckline being higher than the front part of the neckline, greatly improving the fit of the garment. This is followed by the yoke proper, during which stitches are increased in regular intervals. At this point, a multicolored stranded pattern can be incorporated, commonly using no more than two colors per round.

Some of the patterns in this book will at this point require working a few more short rows, which again will elongate the Back yet a little more. After having reached the final yoke height, stitches are distributed a different way for dividing into Body and Sleeves, whereby the sleeve stitches are first placed on hold. Between Front and Back, new underarm stitches are additionally cast on to shape the armhole. Now, the Body is worked in the round to the desired overall length, including the hem ribbing, after which the body stitches are bound off.

For the Sleeves, the formerly held sleeve stitches are now placed onto a double-pointed needle set (or a circular needle for Magic Loop; see page 19). Now, half the required underarm stitches are worked into the corresponding additionally cast-on underarm stitches at the Body, then the Sleeve stitches are worked, and finally, the remaining half of the required underarm stitches are worked into the corresponding additionally cast-on underarm stitches at the Body. To avoid unsightly holes in the underarm area, one extra stitch can be additionally picked up from each armhole edge, which in the following round will be knitted together with the sleeve stitches. Finally, the sleeve, too, is continued in the round. Depending on the design, most sleeves will also include sleeve tapering decreases. When the desired overall length of the sleeve has been reached, including the cuff, all stitches are bound off.

Finally, the ends are woven in, the garment is wet blocked by placing it under moistened towels, and then it is left to dry horizontally.

TIP

The colorwork yoke can easily be wet blocked before dividing for the sleeves if stitches are transferred to a spare needle with long cord or a long piece of sturdy, tear-resistant thread or floss!

Schematic with explanations to measurements:

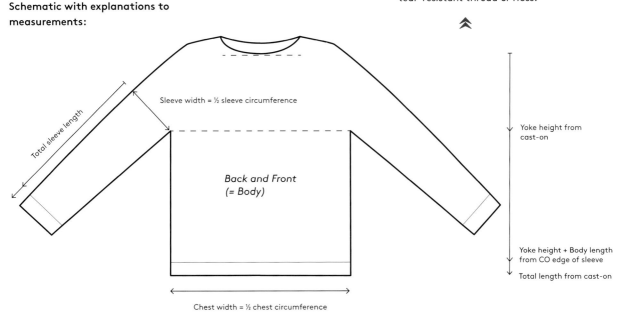

Total sleeve length

Sleeve width = ½ sleeve circumference

Back and Front (= Body)

Yoke height from cast-on

Yoke height + Body length from CO edge of sleeve

Total length from cast-on

Chest width = ½ chest circumference

INCREASES

Increases from the bar between stitches are especially popular, since they blend well into surrounding Stockinette stitch fabric. Often, they are worked to the left *and right of one or more center stitches. In this case, they are worked in pairs, mirror-inverted as a right-leaning and a left-leaning increase.*

LEFT-LEANING INCREASE FROM THE BAR BETWEEN STITCHES (M1L)

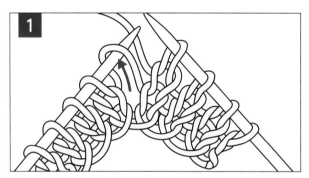

With the tip of the left needle, lift the horizontal bar between the right and left needle from the front.

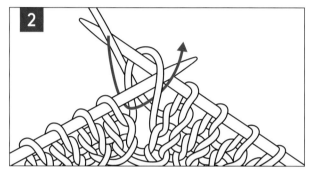

Knit this horizontal bar through the back loop (twisted) …

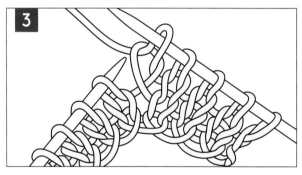

…and let it slide from the left needle.

MNEMONIC

To know which way the lifted bar will slant, this little mnemonic comes in handy: "I've **LEFT** the **FRONT** door open" (bar picked up from the front makes for a left-slanting increase), and "I'll be **RIGHT BACK**" (bar picked up from the back creates a right-slanting increase).

PLEASE NOTE

"Make one left / Make one right": A left-leaning increase from the bar between stitches is called M1L ("make one left"), and a right-leaning increase from the bar between stitches, M1R ("make one right").

RIGHT-LEANING INCREASE FROM THE BAR BETWEEN STITCHES (M1R)

With the tip of the left needle, lift the horizontal bar between the right and left needle from the back.

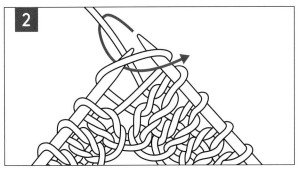

Knit this horizontal bar the regular way (not twisted) ...

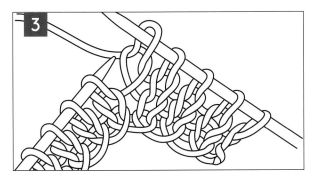

...and let it slide from the left needle.

DECREASES

Decreases can be worked either within the row or at the edge of a knitted piece. In general, the stitch count gets reduced in the appropriate spot by knitting two or more stitches together. Depending on the way the decrease is worked, it will lean either to the right or the left.

RIGHT-LEANING DECREASE: KNITTING 2 STITCHES TOGETHER

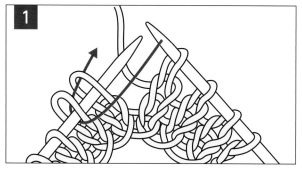

Insert the right needle from left to right first into the stitch after the next one, then into the next stitch on the left needle.

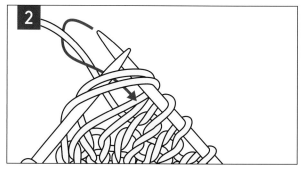

Pull the working yarn through as if to knit.

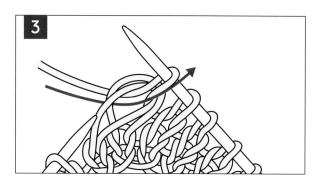

Let both stitches slip from the left needle. Using this method, you can, of course, also knit 3 or more stitches together.

LEFT-LEANING DECREASE: SLIP, KNIT, PASS SLIPPED STITCH OVER (SKP)

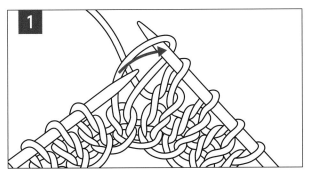

Slip the first stitch as if to knit.

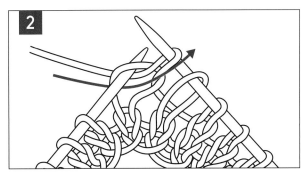

Knit the next stitch.

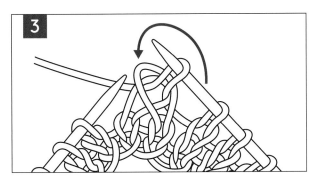

Pass the previously slipped stitch over from right to left and off the needle.

TIP

Another way of knitting two stitches together left-leaning is to first slip both stitches, then knit them together. For this, slip both stitches individually as if to knit, then place them back onto the left needle (so that they they are mounted on the needle the other way around), and knit them together through the back loop.

SHORT ROWS

DOUBLE STITCH

In this technique, a double stitch is worked by slipping the stitch at the turning point after having turned and pulling it away from the viewer. Here, it is important to note that later, both legs of the double stitch are counted and worked off as one stitch.

If the turn happens during a purl row, the first stitch after turning (which in this case will be a knit stitch) is slipped purlwise, too (with working yarn in front of work). Then, the working yarn is pulled over the stitch toward the back (away from the viewer).

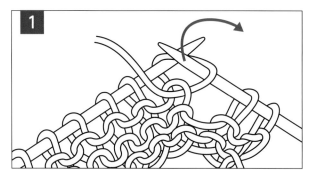

After turning, slip the first stitch as if to purl, with yarn in front of work.

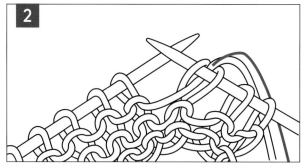

Pull the working yarn over the right needle and over the stitch just worked toward the back (away from the viewer) so that both legs of the stitch are visible.

JOINING PIECES

WHIPSTITCH

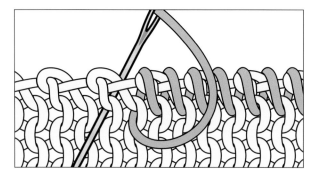

The needle is always led over the edge of the pieces toward the back, then inserted through both layers from the back to the front.

MATTRESS STITCH

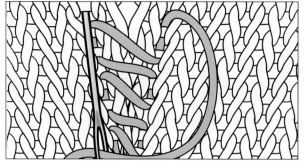

Place the edges of the two pieces to be joined next to each other with their right sides facing up, and insert a tapestry needle under the horizontal strands of two stitches on the left piece, between the selvedge stitch and the first knit stitch. Insert the tapestry needle from the bottom to the top under two horizontal bars of the corresponding stitches on the right piece, and continue in the same way to the end of the seam.

STRANDED COLORWORK PATTERNS

Stranded colorwork patterns are worked using two or more colors in one row or round at the same time. When knitting stranded colorwork, the active color changes constantly within the row or round, working with at least two different strands of yarn at the same time. Colorwork charts show how many stitches have to be worked in which color. Strands in unused colors are carried along in the back of the work, neither too loosely nor too taut.

After every three stitches, the strand in the back has to be locked in. For working stranded colorwork in larger rounds, it is recommended to use the Fair Isle technique with two strands running alongside each other (see illustration). When working in back-and-forth rows, and for sleeves, too, it is advisable to work with one strand only and to cross the colors separately.

HOLDING THE WORKING YARN WHEN KNITTING WITH TWO STRANDS OF YARN

First, the contrasting color is held the regular way as done when working with one color, leading the strand over the base of the index finger. Then, the main color is led over the top of the index finger, held in place between ring finger and pinkie. Now, the strand is lifted once more and led back again counterclockwise (twisted). When then working in main color or contrasting color according to the colorwork chart, the colors will cross automatically on the wrong side of the fabric.

HOLDING THE WORKING YARN WHEN KNITTING WITH THREE STRANDS OF YARN

For knitting with three strands of yarn, i.e., with two contrasting colors in one round, the main color is located at the bottom and in front, followed by contrasting color 1 in the middle, and then contrasting color 2 in the top part of the index finger.

PLEASE NOTE

The strands in unused colors, called floats, are usually carried in the back. Sometimes, they can be used as decorative elements in the pattern, as is the case with Erlendur (see page 37), where they run in front of work over a width of 2 stitches.

BINDING OFF

ELASTIC BIND-OFF

Often, knitting patterns will state to "bind off loosely." In this case, bind off the stitches the regular way with passing over, but make sure to hold the working yarn very loosely. In general, a loosely bound-off edge will have a neater and more even appearance than one that constricts because it

has been bound off too tightly. To avoid problems of this kind, you can use a larger needle size for binding off, which automatically produces larger stitches. As an alternative, there is the following trick:

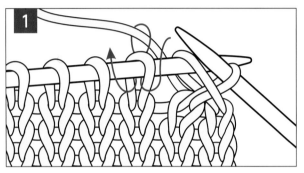

Follow the instructions for regular bind-off with passing over, but, for the time being, still keep the stitch passed over on the left needle. Past it, knit the next stitch.

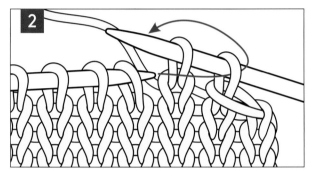

Let the stitch you just worked, together with the stitch formerly passed over and still sitting on the left needle, slide from the left needle.

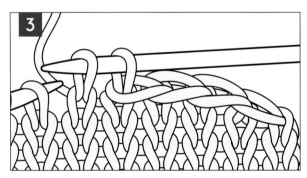

Repeat the working steps from 1 and 2 until all stitches have been bound off. This trick will help you to bind off more loosely.

WORKING IN THE ROUND
WITH MAGIC LOOP

An alternative to double-pointed needles for knitting small circumferences is the magic loop technique. To work magic loop, you need a circular needle with a long cord.

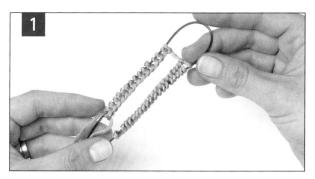

Cast on the required number of stitches and slide them to the middle of the cord. Then, pull out a length of cord in the middle of the stitches of the CO row.

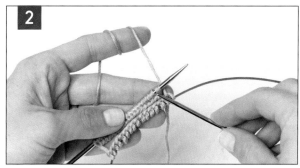

Now, slide the stitches at the beginning of the round (BoR) onto the left needle tip and pull the right needle tip out of the knitting, letting the stitches slide onto the cord. Begin working the round, making sure that the cast-on is not twisted.

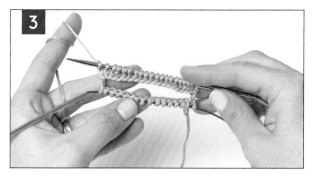

After having knitted all the stitches on the left needle (now transferred to the right needle), slide these stitches to the middle of the cord and the other stitches onto the left needle tip.

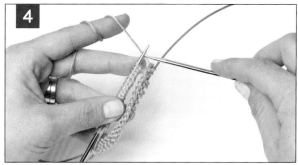

Work in increments of half a round in this way before adjusting again.

KNITTING SOCKS WITH BOOMERANG HEEL
BASIC INSTRUCTIONS FOR SOCKS WORKED IN STOCKINETTE STITCH

Work cast-on, cuff, and leg according to pattern instructions.

Boomerang Heel

When the correct leg length has been reached, begin working the heel.

After having completed the last round of the leg, work the stitches of needles 1, 2, and 3. Now, transfer the stitches of needles 2 and 3 onto a stitch holder or piece of waste yarn.

Divide the stitches of needles 4 and 1 into three parts: one middle part, bordered by two outer parts. The two outer parts should have an equal stitch count. Now, work short rows with double stitch from the outside toward the middle (rows getting shorter) as follows:

Row 1 (RS): Knit all sts of needles 4 and 1, turn work.

Row 2 (WS): Pull out a double stitch (see page 16), purl all sts of needles 1 and 4, turn work.

Row 3 (RS): Pull out a double stitch, knit all sts up to the double stitch at the end of the row, but do not work the double stitch itself. Turn work.

Row 4 (WS): Pull out a double stitch, purl all sts up to the double stitch at the end of the row, but do not work the double stitch itself. Turn work.

Repeat Rows 3 and 4 until all stitches of the two outer sections have turned into double stitches; the stitches of the middle section have remained regular stitches.

Now work two rounds over the stitches on all four needles, as follows. During the first one of these two in-between-rounds, knit together both legs of the double stitch at the same time (as you would for k2tog) when you encounter them. Then knit one more round.

Now, work short rows again, but this time from the middle out (rows getting longer).

Row 1 (RS): Knit the stitches of the middle section, turn work.

Row 2 (WS): Pull out a double stitch. Purl the stitches of the middle section, turn work.

Row 3 (RS): Pull out a double stitch. Knit up to the double stitch of the previous row, knit the double stitch (knit both legs of the double stitch together as in k2tog), then knit the following stitch. Turn work.

Row 4 (WS): Pull out a double stitch. Purl up to the double stitch of the previous row, purl the double stitch (purl both legs of the double stitch together as in p2tog), then purl the following stitch. Turn work.

Repeat Rows 3 and 4 until all stitches of the two outer sections have turned into double stitches; the stitches of the middle section have remained regular stitches.

The last RS row is at the same time the beginning of the first round of the foot.

Foot

Continue working stockinette stitch in the round up to the beginning of the toe decreases.

Toe Decreases

When the required length has been reached, work toe decreases as follows:

Round 1: Knit all stitches.

Round 2: On needle 1, knit to the last 3 sts, k2tog (third-to-last stitch with next-to-last stitch), then knit the last stitch. Of the stitches on needle 2, knit the first stitch, slip the next stitch, knit the following stitch, and pass the slipped stitch over the knitted one. Knit all remaining stitches. Work the stitches of needle 3 as done for needle 1 and the stitches of needle 4 as done for needle 2.

Round 3: Knit all stitches.

Round 4: Work the same as Round 2.

Work all following rounds as done for Round 2, until only 8 stitches remain in all.

FINISHING

Break the working yarn, and pull it through the remaining stitches, then secure. Weave in all ends.

ABBREVIATIONS

BO	=	bind off	M1R	=	make one right-leaning increase from the bar between stitches (see pg 13)
BoR	=	beginning of the round			
CC	=	contrasting color			
CO	=	cast on	MC	=	main color
ctr st	=	center stitch	rep	=	repeat
dec	=	decrease(d)	rnd (s)	=	round (s)
DPN(s)	=	double-pointed needle(s)	RS	=	right side of work
DSt	=	double stitch(es)	skp	=	slip, knit, pass (see pg 15)
inc	=	increase(d)	sl	=	slip
m	=	stitch marker	st(s)	=	stitch(es)
M1L	=	make one left-leaning increase from the bar between stitches (see pg 12)	st st	=	stockinette stitch
			tog	=	knit or purl together
			WS	=	wrong side of work

Sweaters

STEINUNN

Sweater in a stranded colorwork pattern

♦♦♦

Loose Fit
Shown in size S.

SIZES

S, M, L, XL

Positive ease of at least 7.1 in. (18 cm) has already been incorporated.

PLEASE NOTE: Numbers for individual sizes are listed in order from smallest to largest size, divided by slashes. If only one number is given, it applies to all sizes.

Chest circumference: 41/44.1/47.2/50.4 in. (104/112/120/128 cm)

Sleeve width: 6.5/6.7/6.9/7.1 in. (16.5/17/17.5/18 cm)

MATERIALS

◆ Lana Grossa Alta Moda Alpaca; #4 medium weight; 90% alpaca, 5% pure new wool, 5% polyamide; 153 yd. (140 m) per 1.75 oz. (50 g); 10/11/12/13 skeins #36 Petrol/Royal Meliert (Petrol/Royal Heathered), and 1 skein each #14 Rohweiß (Natural White) and #15 Grau/Beige Meliert (Gray/Beige Heathered)

PLEASE NOTE: Check the ball bands, and only use skeins of the same dye lot together. Actual total yardage may vary, depending on individual knitting style.

◆ 2 circular needles size US 6 (4.0 mm), 16 in. (40 cm) and 32 in. (80 cm) long

◆ circular needle size US 7 (4.5 mm), 24 in. (60 cm) long

◆ 2 circular needles size US 10 (6.0 mm), 24 in. (60 cm) and 32 in. (80 cm) long

◆ DPN sets size US 6 (4.0 mm) and US 7 (4.5 mm)

◆ tapestry needle for weaving in ends

◆ stitch markers

◆ stitch holders or waste yarn

GAUGE

Stockinette stitch in one color on US 7 (4.5 mm) needles: 20 sts and 28 rows/rnds = 4 x 4 in. (10 x 10 cm)

PLEASE NOTE: Since everybody knits differently, the stranded colorwork pattern should be swatched to determine whether a smaller or larger needle size might be required to match the listed gauge. Needle size US 10 (6.0 mm) is recommended.

COLOR DESIGNATIONS

MC: Petrol/Royal Heathered

CC1: Natural White

CC2: Gray/Beige Heathered

STITCH PATTERNS

Ribbing pattern in the round
Alternate k2, p2 to end of round.

Stockinette stitch in the round
Knit all stitches in all rounds.

Stranded colorwork pattern in the round

Work all rounds in st st, following the appropriate chart. Repeat the pattern repeat throughout the round.

Colorwork Chart 1: The pattern repeat is 6 sts wide. Work Rounds 1–6 once.

Colorwork Chart 2: The pattern repeat is initially 8 sts wide. Work Rounds 1–4 once. In Round 3, increase as shown.

Colorwork Chart 3: The pattern repeat is initially 15 sts wide. Work Rounds 1–20 once. In Rounds 3, 8, and 15, increase as shown.

Colorwork Chart 4: The pattern repeat is 16 sts wide. Work Rounds 1–25 once.

PLEASE NOTE: Lock in floats after every 3rd stitch. Keep CC at the base of the finger, i.e., in front.

TIP

First, read through all the instructions and mark all numbers pertaining to the size you want to knit. This way, you are prepared in advance and don't have to search for the correct numbers while knitting.

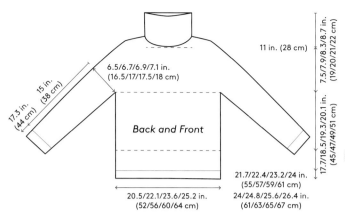

6.5/6.7/6.9/7.1 in.
(16.5/17/17.5/18 cm)

11 in. (28 cm)

15 in.
(38 cm)

17.3 in.
(44 cm)

7.5/7.9/8.3/8.7 in.
(19/20/21/22 cm)

17.7/18.5/19.3/20.1 in.
(45/47/49/51 cm)

Back and Front

21.7/22.4/23.2/24 in.
(55/57/59/61 cm)

20.5/22.1/23.6/25.2 in.
(52/56/60/64 cm)

24/24.8/25.6/26.4 in.
(61/63/65/67 cm)

INSTRUCTIONS

Using shorter circular needle in size US 6 (4.0 mm) and MC, CO 125/125/130/130 sts. Join in the round and place a marker for the BoR (middle of the Back).

Next round: Rep [k3, p2] around.

Continue working rounds of "k3, p2" until piece has reached 6.3 in. (16 cm) overall height, then work decreases as follows: rep [k1, skp, p2] to end of round (= 100/100/104/104 sts).

Continue in ribbing pattern. When piece has reached 11 in. (28 cm) overall height, change to circular needle in size US 7 (4.5 mm), and knit 1 rnd.

Now, work first inc rnd:

Sizes S and M:

Inc Rnd 1: K2, [k3, M1L] 32 times, k2 (= 132 sts).

Sizes L and XL:

Inc Rnd 1: K1, [k3, M1L] 34 times, k1 (= 138 sts).

All Sizes:

Work short rows as follows:

Row 1 (RS): Beginning at the BoR (center back), k44/46/48/50, turn work.

Row 2 (WS): DSt, purl to center back, p44/46/48/50 more, turn work.

Row 3 (RS): DSt, knit to 3 sts after the last DSt, knitting both legs of the DSt as one when you encounter it, turn work.

Row 4 (WS): DSt, purl to 3 sts after the last DSt, purling both legs of the DSt together as one, turn work.

Rep the last two rows (Rows 3 and 4) once, for a total of 3 DSts worked on each side.

Then knit for 2 rnds, working both legs of the DSt as one in the first rnd.

Change to short circular needle in size US 10 (6.0 mm). Work in stranded pattern from Colorwork Chart 1. Work the pattern repeat [6 sts wide] 22/22/23/23 times per round (= 132/132/138/138 sts), work Rnds 1–6 once.

Work Inc Rnds 2 and 3 in MC as follows:

Size S:

Inc Rnd 2: *K3, M1L, rep from * to end of rnd (= 176 sts).

Inc Rnd 3: *K11, M1L, rep from * to end of rnd (= 192 sts).

Size M:

Inc Rnd 2: *K2, M1L, rep from * to end of rnd (= 198 sts).

Inc Rnd 3: K4, [k19, M1L] 10 times, k4 (= 208 sts).

Size L:

Inc Rnd 2: *K3, M1L, rep from * to end of rnd (= 184 sts).

Inc Rnd 3: *K6, [k4, M1L] 20 times, k6, rep from * once (= 224 sts).

Size XL:

Inc Rnd 2: *K2, M1L, rep from * to end of rnd (= 207 sts).

Inc Rnd 3: K5, [k6, M1L] 33 times, k4 (= 240 sts).

All Sizes:

Work in stranded colorwork pattern from Colorwork Chart 2. Work the pattern repeat [8 sts wide] 24/26/28/30 times per round (= 192/208/224/240 sts), work Rnds 1–4 once, at the same time increasing in Rnd 3 as shown in Chart 2; from Rnd 4 on, work the pattern repeat [now 9 sts wide] 24/26/28/30 times per round (= 216/234/252/270 sts).

Now, work Inc Rnd 4 in MC as follows:

Size S:

Inc Rnd 4: *K24, M1L, rep from * to end of rnd (= 225 sts).

Size M:

Inc Rnd 4: *K39, M1L, rep from * to end of rnd (= 240 sts).

Size L:

Inc Rnd 4: *K84, M1L, rep from * to end of rnd (= 255 sts).

Size XL:

In MC, work 1 rnd even without increases (= 270 sts).

All Sizes:

Work in stranded pattern from Colorwork Chart 3. Work the pattern repeat [15 sts wide] 15/16/17/18 times per round (= 225/240/255/270 sts), work Rnds 1–20 once, at the same time increasing in Rnds 3, 8, and 15 as stated = after Rnd 20, there will be 15/16/17/18 pattern repeats [now 20 sts wide] worked per rnd (= 300/320/340/360 sts). If needed, change to longer circular needle in size US 10 (6.0 mm) to accommodate the larger stitch count.

After having completed the colorwork pattern, break the working yarn in CC. Change to circular needle in size US 7 (4.5 mm) and, if needed, continue in st st in MC, until an overall height of 7.5/7.9/8.3/8.7 in. (19/20/21/22 cm) from center front AFTER Turtleneck (ribbing pattern) (i.e., measured from first st st rnd) has been reached. Then divide sts for Body and Sleeves as follows:

Starting at center back, k47/51/55/59 for the Back, place 56/58/60/62 Sleeve sts on holder, CO 5 new sts, place m (= new BoR), CO 5 new sts, k94/102/110/118 for the Front, place 56/58/60/62 Sleeve sts on holder, CO 10 new underarm sts, k47/51/55/59 Back sts to center back.

You now have 56/58/60/62 sts + 10 sts for each Sleeve. Front and Back each have 94/102/110/118 sts + 20 sts = total Body sts = 208/224/240/256 sts.

Continue with circular needle in size US 7 (4.5 mm) in MC in st st, working until Body measures 10.2/10.7/11/11.4 in. (26/27/28/29 cm) from Sleeve. Change to longer circular needle in size US 10 (6.0 mm).

Work in stranded pattern from Colorwork Chart 4. Work the pattern repeat [16 sts wide] 13/14/15/16 times per round (= 208/224/240/256 sts), work Rnds 1–25 once.

When piece has reached a height of 21.7/22.5/23.2/24 in. (55/57/59/61 cm) at center front AFTER the turtleneck (ribbing pattern), i.e., measured from first st st rnd, change to long circular needle in size US 6 (4.0 mm), and work 2.4 in. (6 cm) in ribbing pattern. Bind off all sts using elastic BO method. The overall height at center front AFTER the turtleneck is 24/24.8/25.6/26.4 in. (61/63/65/67 cm).

SLEEVES (MAKE 2)

PLEASE NOTE: To avoid unsightly holes, 1 additional (unlisted) stitch should be picked up at each side of the armhole. In the following round, knit each of the 2 extra sts together with the corresponding Sleeve stitch to return to the original stitch count.

Take up the formerly held 56/58/60/62 Sleeve sts with a DPN set in size US 7 (4.5 mm), and continue in MC in st st: For the armhole, beginning at the center of the additionally CO sts of the Body, work 5 sts (+ 1 additionally picked up st for hole prevention) for the Sleeve into the corresponding sts at the Body; knit the Sleeve sts; work 5 sts (+ 1 additionally picked up st for hole prevention) for the Sleeve into the corresponding additionally CO Body/Sleeve sts, place m (= BoR); in the following round, knit the 2 extra sts together with the adjoining sts as described above (= 66/68/70/72 sts).

When piece has reached 3.2 in. (8 cm) from begin of Sleeve, work first sleeve tapering dec rnd as follows: k2, k2tog, k to 4 sts before m, skp, k2 (= 2 sts decreased = 64/66/68/70 sts).

Repeat sleeve tapering decreases in every 11th/10th/11th/10th rnd a total of 7/8/7/8 times (= 50/50/54/54 sts).

Continue in st st in the round until Sleeve either measures approx. 15 in. (38 cm) or is 2.4 in. (6 cm) shorter than desired length. Change to DPN set in size US 6 (4.0 mm), and work 2.4 in. (6 cm) in ribbing pattern in MC. Bind off all sts using elastic BO method.

FINISHING

Neatly weave in all ends. Turn the garment inside out, gently pin it into shape on an even horizontal surface, cover it with a moistened cloth, and let it dry.

COLORWORK CHART 3

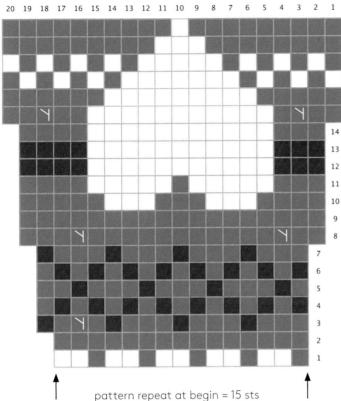

pattern repeat at begin = 15 sts

COLORWORK CHART 1

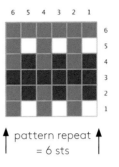

pattern repeat
= 6 sts

COLORWORK CHART 4

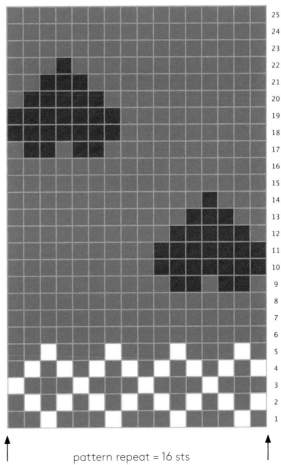

pattern repeat = 16 sts

COLORWORK CHART 2

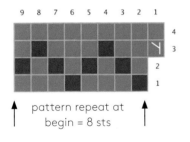

pattern repeat at
begin = 8 sts

LEGEND

= MC: Petrol/Royal Heathered

= CC1: Natural White

= CC2: Gray/Beige Heathered

= M1L

HILDUR
Sweater in a stranded colorwork pattern

◆◆◆

Regular Fit
Shown in size S.

SIZES

S, M, L, XL

Positive ease of approx. 5.5 in. (14 cm) has already been incorporated.

PLEASE NOTE: Numbers for individual sizes are listed in order from smallest to largest size, divided by slashes. If only one number is given, it applies to all sizes.

Chest circumference: 37.8/41/45/48 in. (96/104/114/122 cm)

Sleeve width: 5.5/6.1/6.5/7.1 in. (14/15.5/16.5/18 cm)

MATERIALS

◆ Lana Grossa Alta Moda Alpaca; #4 medium weight; 90% alpaca, 5% pure new wool, 5% polyamide; 153 yd. (140 m) per 1.75 oz. (50 g); 8/9/10/11 skeins #10 Mokka Meliert (Mocha Heathered) and 1 skein each #14 Rohweiß (Natural White) and #15 Grau/Beige Meliert (Gray/Beige Heathered)

PLEASE NOTE: Check the ball bands, and only use skeins of the same dye lot together. Actual total yardage may vary, depending on individual knitting style.

◆ 2 circular needles size US 6 (4.0 mm), 16 in. (40 cm) and 32 in. (80 cm) long

◆ circular needle size US 7 (4.5 mm), 24 in. (60 cm) long

◆ 2 circular needles size US 10 (6.0 mm), 24 in. (60 cm) and 32 in. (80 cm) long

◆ DPN sets sizes US 6 (4.0 mm), US 7 (4.5 mm), and US 10 (6.0 mm)

◆ tapestry needle for weaving in ends

◆ stitch markers

◆ stitch holders or waste yarn

GAUGE

Stockinette stitch in one color on size US 7 (4.5 mm) needles: 20 sts and 28 rows/rounds = 4 x 4 in. (10 x 10 cm)

PLEASE NOTE: Since everybody knits differently, the stranded colorwork pattern should be swatched to determine whether a smaller or larger needle size might be required to match the listed gauge. Needle size US 10 (6.0 mm) is recommended.

COLOR DESIGNATIONS

MC: Mocha Heathered

CC1: Natural White

CC2: Gray/Beige Heathered

STITCH PATTERNS

Ribbing pattern in the round

Alternate "k2, p2" to end of round.

Stockinette stitch in the round

Knit all stitches in all rounds.

Stranded colorwork pattern in the round

Work all rnds in st st according to the colorwork chart. Repeat the pattern repeat [initially 8 sts wide] throughout the round. Work Rnds 1–36 once, increasing in Rnds 7, 13, 24, and 29 as shown.

PLEASE NOTE: Lock in floats after every 3rd stitch. Keep CC at the base of the finger, i.e., in front.

TIP

First, read through all the instructions and mark all numbers pertaining to the size you want to knit. This way, you are prepared in advance and don't have to search for the correct numbers while knitting.

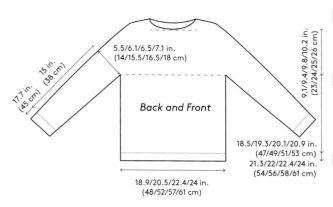

5.5/6.1/6.5/7.1 in.
(14/15.5/16.5/18 cm)

15 in.
(38 cm)

17.7 in.
(45 cm)

Back and Front

9.1/9.4/9.8/10.2 in.
(23/24/25/26 cm)

18.5/19.3/20.1/20.9 in.
(47/49/51/53 cm)
21.3/22/22.4/24 in.
(54/56/58/61 cm)

18.9/20.5/22.4/24 in.
(48/52/57/61 cm)

INSTRUCTIONS

Using shorter circular needle in size US 6 (4.0 mm) and CC2, CO 96/96/100/100 sts. Join in the round and place a marker for the BoR (middle of the Back). Work 3.2 in. (8 cm) in ribbing pattern.

Now, work first inc rnd as follows:

Sizes S and M:

Inc Rnd 1: K3, [k3, M1L] 30 times, k3 (= 126 sts).

Work 2 rnds in st st.

Sizes L and XL:

Inc Rnd 1: K2, [k3, M1L] 32 times, k2 (= 132 sts).

Work 2 rnds in st st.

All Sizes:

Work short rows as follows:

Row 1 (RS): Beginning at the BoR (center back), k40/42/44/46 sts, turn work.

Row 2 (WS): DSt, purl to center back, p40/42/44/46 sts, turn work.

Row 3 (RS): DSt, knit to 3 sts after the last DSt, knitting both legs of the DSt as one when you encounter it, turn work.

Row 4 (WS): DSt, purl to 3 sts after the last DSt, purling both legs of the DSt together as one, turn work.

Rep the last two rows (Rows 3 and 4) once, for a total of 3 DSts worked on each side.

Knit for 2 rnds, working both legs of the DSt as one in the first rnd.

Then, work Inc Rnds 2 and 3 as follows:

Size S:

Inc Rnd 2: K1, [k4, M1L] 31 times, k1 (= 157 sts).

Inc Rnd 3: K1, [k52, M1L] 3 times (= 160 sts).

Size M:

Inc Rnd 2: [K3, M1L] 42 times (= 168 sts).

Inc Rnd 3: [K21, M1L] 8 times (= 176 sts).

Size L:

Inc Rnd 2: *K3, M1L, rep from * to end of rnd (= 176 sts).

Inc Rnd 3: *K11, M1L, rep from * to end of rnd (= 192 sts).

Size XL:

Inc Rnd 2: *K2, M1L, rep from * to end of rnd (= 198 sts).

Inc Rnd 3: K4, [k19, M1L] 10 times, k4 (= 208 sts).

All Sizes:

Change to short circular needle in size US 10 (6.0 mm). Work stranded colorwork pattern from colorwork chart. Work the pattern repeat [initially 8 sts wide] 20/22/24/26 times per round (= 160/176/192/208 sts). Work Rnds 1–36 once, increasing in Rnds 7, 13, 24, and 29 as shown. After Rnd 29, the pattern repeat [now 14 sts wide] will be worked 20/22/24/26 times per round (= 280/308/336/364 sts). If needed, change to longer circular needle in size US 10 (6.0 mm) to accommodate the larger stitch count.

After having completed the colorwork pattern, break the working yarn in CC, change to circular needle in US size 7 (4.5 mm) and, if needed, continue in st st in MC, until an overall height of 9/9.5/9.8/10.2 in. (23/24/25/26 cm) from CO on center front has been reached. Then, divide sts for Sleeves and Body as follows:

Starting at center back, k45/49/54/58 Back sts, place 50/56/60/66 Sleeve sts on holder, CO 3 new sts, place m (= new BoR), CO 3 new sts, k90/98/108/116 Front sts, place 50/56/60/66 Sleeve sts on holder, CO 6 new sts, k45/49/54/58 Back sts to center back.

You now have 50/56/60/66 sts + 6 sts = 56/62/66/72 sts for each Sleeve. Front and Back each have 90/98/108/116 sts + 12 sts = 192/208/228/244 total Body sts on the needles.

Continue with circular needle in size US 7 (4.5 mm) in MC in st st, working until Body measures 9.5/9.8/10.2/10.7 in. (24/25/26/27 cm) from Sleeve. Now, change to long circular needle in size US 6 (4.0 mm), and work 2.8 in. (7 cm) in ribbing pattern. Bind off all sts, using elastic BO method.

SLEEVES (MAKE 2)

PLEASE NOTE: To avoid unsightly holes, 1 additional (unlisted) stitch should be picked up at each side of the armhole. In the following round, knit each of the 2 extra sts together with the corresponding Sleeve st to return to the original stitch count.

Take up the formerly held 50/56/60/66 Sleeve sts with a DPN set in size US 7 (4.5 mm), and continue in MC in st st: For the armhole, beginning at the center of the additionally CO sts of the Body, work 3 sts (+ 1 additionally picked up st for hole prevention) for the Sleeve into the corresponding sts at the Body; knit the Sleeve sts; into the corresponding additionally CO sts at the Body, work 3 sts (+ 1 additionally picked up st for hole prevention) for the Sleeve, place m (= BoR); in the following round, knit the 2 extra sts together with the adjoining sts as described above (= 56/62/66/72 sts).

For sleeve tapering, at 3.1 in. (8 cm) height from begin of Sleeve, work first dec rnd as follows: k2, k2tog, knit to 4 sts before m, skp, k2 (= 2 sts decreased = 54/60/64/70 sts).

Repeat decreases in every 24th/12th/18th/11th rnd a total of 3/6/4/7 times (= 48/48/56/56 sts).

Continue in st st in the round until Sleeve either measures approx. 15 in. (38 cm) or is 2.8 in. (7 cm) shorter than desired length.

Change to DPN set in size US 10 (6.0 mm) and, working in MC and CC1 for the small stranded colorwork pattern, work Rnds 8–12 of the colorwork chart. Repeat the pattern repeat [8 sts wide] throughout the round.

Afterwards, change to DPN set in size US 7 (4.5 mm) and work 2 rnds more in MC in st st.

Change to DPN set in size US 6 (4.0 mm) and work in ribbing pattern for 2 in. (5 cm). Bind off all sts, using elastic BO method.

FINISHING

Fold the collar inward and, using a strand of working yarn in MC, sew down all around in whipstitch.

Neatly weave in all ends. Turn the garment inside out, gently pin it into shape on an even horizontal surface, cover it with a moistened cloth, and let it dry.

LEGEND

= MC: Mocha Heathered

= CC1: Natural White

= CC2: Gray/Beige Heathered

= M1L

COLORWORK CHART

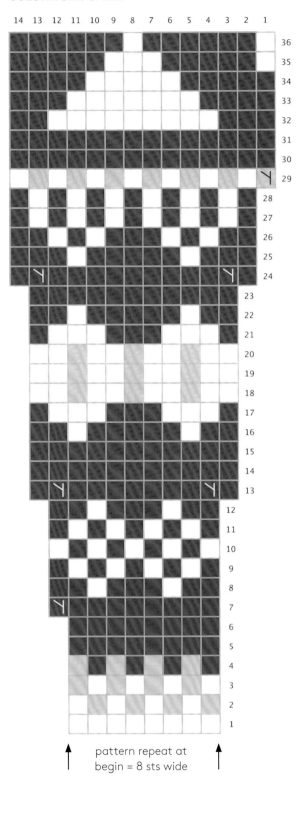

pattern repeat at begin = 8 sts wide

ERLENDUR
Sweater in a stranded colorwork pattern

◆◆◆

SIZES

S, M, L, XL

Positive ease of approx. 5.5 in. (14 cm) has already been incorporated.

PLEASE NOTE: Numbers for individual sizes are listed in order from smallest to largest size, divided by slashes. If only one number is given, it applies to all sizes.

Chest circumference: 40/42/45/50 in. (100/106/115/126 cm)

Sleeve width: 5.9/6.5/6.9/7.3 in. (15/16.5/17.5/18.5 cm)

MATERIALS

◆ ggh Norvika; #5 bulky weight; 30% Norwegian wool, 30% acrylic, 20% alpaca, 13% bio-polyamide: Bio-feel®, 7% polyamide; 70 yd. (65 m) per 1.75 oz. (50 g); 9/10/11/12 skeins #05 Dunkelblau (Dark Blue) and 1/1/1/2 skeins #029 Wollweiß (Natural White)

PLEASE NOTE: Check the ball bands, and only use skeins of the same dye lot together. Actual total yardage may vary, depending on individual knitting style.

◆ 2 circular needles size US 6 (4.0 mm), 16 in. (40 cm) and 32 in. (80 cm) long

◆ 2 circular needles size US 7 (4.5 mm), 16 in. (40 cm) and 24 in. (60 cm) long

◆ 2 circular needles size US 10.5 (6.5 mm), 24 in. (60 cm) and 32 in. (80 cm) long

◆ DPN sets in US 6 (4.0 mm) and US 7 (4.5 mm)

◆ tapestry needle for weaving in ends

◆ stitch markers

◆ stitch holders or waste yarn

GAUGE

Stockinette stitch in one color on size US 7 (4.5 mm) needles: 14 sts and 18 rows/rounds = 4 x 4 in. (10 x 10 cm)

PLEASE NOTE: Since everybody knits differently, the two-color stranded pattern should be swatched to determine whether a smaller or larger needle size might be required to match the listed gauge. Needle size US 10.5 (6.5 mm) is recommended.

COLOR DESIGNATIONS

MC: Dark Blue

CC: Natural White

STITCH PATTERNS

Ribbing pattern in the round

Alternate "k2, p2" to end of round.

Stockinette stitch in the round

Knit all stitches in all rounds.

Stranded colorwork pattern in the round

Work all rnds in st st, following the appropriate chart. Repeat the pattern repeat [initially 10 sts wide] throughout the round.

Charts for sizes S and M: Work Rnds 1–29 once, increasing in Rnds 3, 8, 14, and 22 as stated, and in Rnds 17–19, keeping the floats in front of work as shown.

Charts for sizes L and XL: Work Rnds 1–35 once, increasing in Rnds 3, 8, 16, and 26 as stated, and in Rnds 20–23, keeping the floats in front of work as shown.

PLEASE NOTE: Lock in floats after every 3rd stitch. Keep CC at the base of the finger, i.e., in front.

TIP

First, read through all the instructions and mark all numbers pertaining to the size you want to knit. This way, you are prepared in advance and don't have to search for the correct numbers while knitting.

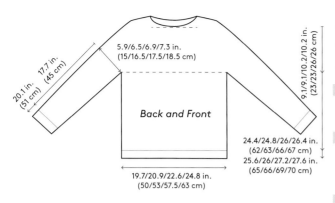

Back and Front

5.9/6.5/6.9/7.3 in.
(15/16.5/17.5/18.5 cm)

17.7 in.
(45 cm)

20.1 in.
(51 cm)

9.1/9.1/10.2/10.2 in.
(23/23/26/26 cm)

24.4/24.8/26/26.4 in.
(62/63/66/67 cm)

25.6/26/27.2/27.6 in.
(65/66/69/70 cm)

19.7/20.9/22.6/24.8 in.
(50/53/57.5/63 cm)

INSTRUCTIONS

Using DPN set in size US 6 (4.0 mm) and MC, CO 56/56/60/60 sts. Join in the round and place a marker for the BoR (middle of the Back). Work 6 rnds in ribbing pattern.

Change to short circular needle in size US 7 (4.5 mm), and knit 1 rnd.

Now, for sizes S and M, work Inc Rnd 1; for sizes L and XL, work Inc Rnds 1 and 2 as follows:

Sizes S and M:

Inc Rnd 1: *K2, M1L, rep from * to end of rnd (= 84 sts).

Work 2 rnds in st st.

Sizes L and XL:

Inc Rnd 1: *K2, M1L, rep from * to end of rnd (= 90 sts).

Work 1 rnd in st st.

Inc Rnd 2: K1, [k4, M1L] 22 times, k1 (= 112 sts).

All Sizes:

Work short rows as follows:

Row 1 (RS): Beginning at the BoR (center back), k26/28/30/32, turn work.

Row 2 (WS): DSt, purl to center back, purl an additional 26/28/30/32 sts, turn work.

Row 3 (RS): DSt, knit to 3 sts after the last DSt, knitting both legs of the DSt as one when you encounter it, turn work.

Row 4 (WS): DSt, purl to 3 sts after the last DSt, purling both legs of the DSt together as one, turn work.

Rep the last two rows (Rows 3 and 4) once, for a total of 3 DSts worked on each side.

Knit for 2 rnds, working both legs of the DSt as one in the first rnd.

Then, for sizes S and M, work Inc Rnd 2; for sizes L and XL, work Inc Rnd 3 as follows:

Size S:

Inc Rnd 2: K3, [k3, M1L] 26 times, k3 (= 110 sts).

Size M:

Inc Rnd 2: * K4, [k2, M1L] 18 times, rep from * once, k4 (= 120 sts).

Size L:

Inc Rnd 3: K2, [k6, M1L] 18 times, k2 (= 130 sts).

Size XL:

Inc Rnd 3: *K4, M1L, rep from * to end of rnd (= 140 sts).

All Sizes:

Change to circular needle in size US 10.5 (6.5 mm). Work the stranded colorwork pattern from the appropriate colorwork chart for your size. Work the pattern repeat [initially 10 sts wide] 11/12/13/14 times per round (= 110/120/130/140 sts). For sizes S and M, work Rnds 1–29 once, increasing in Rnds 3, 8, 16, and 22 as stated, and in Rnds 17–19, keeping the floats in front of work as shown. For sizes L and XL, work Rnds 1–35 once, increasing in Rnds 3, 8, 16, and 26 as stated, and in Rnds 20–23, keeping the floats in front of work as shown. After all increases have been worked, there will be 11/12/13/14 pattern repeats [18 sts wide] to be worked per round (= 198/216/234/252 sts).

After having completed the colorwork pattern, break the working yarn in CC, change to circular needle in size US 7 (4.5 mm) and, if needed, continue in st st in MC until an overall height of 9/9/10.2/10.2 in. (23/23/26/26 cm) from cast-on center front has been reached. Then divide sts for Body and Sleeves as follows, working in MC:

Starting at center back, k32/34/38/41 Back sts, place 35/40/41/44 Sleeve sts on holder, CO 3/3/4/4 new sts, place m (= new BoR), CO 3/3/4/4 new sts, k64/68/76/82 Front sts, place 35/40/41/44 Sleeve sts on holder, CO 6/6/8/8 new sts, k32/34/38/41 Back sts to center back.

You now have 35/40/41/44 sts + 6/6/8/8 sts = 41/46/49/52 sts for each Sleeve. Front and Back each have 64/68/74/82 sts + 12/12/16/16 sts = 140/148/164/180 total Body sts.

Continue, working in MC in st st until Body measures 15.4/15.7/15.7/16.1 in. (39/40/40/41 cm) from Sleeve. Now, change to circular needle in size US 6 (4.0 mm), and work 6 rnds in ribbing pattern. Bind off all sts using elastic BO method.

SLEEVES (MAKE 2)

PLEASE NOTE: To avoid unsightly holes, 1 additional (unlisted) stitch should be picked up at each side of the armhole. In the following round, knit each of the 2 extra sts together with the corresponding Sleeve stitch to return to the original stitch count.

Take up the formerly held 35/40/41/44 Sleeve sts with a DPN set in size US 7 (4.5 mm), and continue in MC in st st: For the armhole, beginning at the center of the additionally CO sts of the Body, work 3/3/4/4 sts (+ 1 additionally picked up st for hole prevention as noted) for the Sleeve into the corresponding sts at the Body; knit the Sleeve sts; into the corresponding additionally CO sts at the Body, work 3/3/4/4 sts (+ 1 additionally picked up st for hole prevention) for the Sleeve, place m (= BoR); in the following round, knit the 2 extra sts together with the adjoining sts as described above (= 41/46/49/52 sts). Adjust stitch counts for sizes S and L by increasing 1 st for each size (= 42/46/50/52 sts).

Continue in st st in the round, working until the Sleeve measures 3.1 in. (8 cm) from begin of Sleeve. Now, work first dec rnd as follows: k2, k2tog, knit to 4 sts before m, skp, k2 (= 2 sts decreased = 40/44/48/50 sts).

Repeat decreases in every 14th/10th/1st/9th rnd 4/6/6/7 times more (= 32/32/36/36 sts).

Continue in st st in the round, working until Sleeve either measures approx. 17.7 in. (45 cm) or is 2.4 in. (6 cm) shorter than desired length. Change to size US 7 (4.5 mm) needles, and work 12 more rnds in ribbing pattern. Bind off all sts, using elastic BO method.

FINISHING

Neatly weave in all ends. Turn the garment inside out, gently pin it into shape on an even horizontal surface, cover it with a moistened cloth, and let it dry.

COLORWORK CHART SIZE L/XL

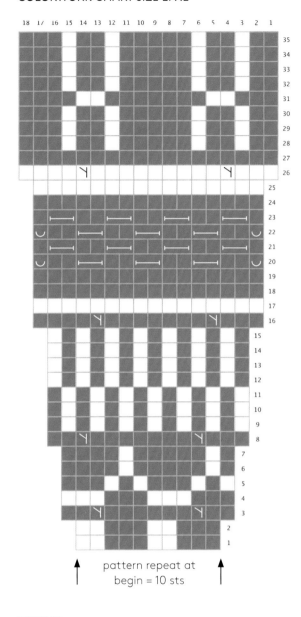

pattern repeat at
begin = 10 sts

COLORWORK CHART SIZE S/M

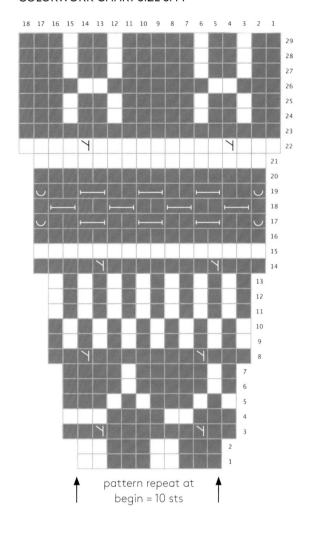

pattern repeat at
begin = 10 sts

LEGEND

= MC: Dark Blue

= CC: Natural White

= M1L

= keep floats in front of work over a width of 2 sts

= keep floats in front of work over a width of 1 st

HALLA
Sweater in a stranded colorwork pattern

◆◆◆

Regular Fit

Shown in size M

SIZES

S, M, L, XL

Positive ease of approx. 5.5 in. (14 cm) has already been incorporated.

PLEASE NOTE: Numbers for individual sizes are listed in order from smallest to largest size, divided by slashes. If only one number is given, it applies to all sizes.

Chest circumference: 40.2/41.7/45.7/47.2 in. (102/106/116/120 cm)

Sleeve width: 5.7/6.3/6.9/7.5 in. (14.5/16/17.5/19 cm)

MATERIALS

◆ Hey Mama Wolf Schafwolle No. 03; #4 medium weight; 100% organic wool; 284 yd. (260 m) per 3.5 oz. (100 g); 4/4/5/5 skeins Krapp (Crimson) and 1 skein Seabird

PLEASE NOTE: Check the ball bands, and only use skeins of the same dye lot together. Actual total yardage may vary, depending on individual knitting style.

◆ 2 circular needles size US 2.5 (3.0 mm), 16 in. (40 cm) and 32 in. (80 cm) long

◆ 2 circular needles size US 4 (3.5 mm), 24 in. (60 cm) and 32 in. (80 cm) long

◆ circular needle size US 6 (4.0 mm), 32 in. (80 cm) long

◆ DPN sets in sizes US 2.5 (3.0 mm), US 4 (3.5 mm), and US 6 (4.0 mm)

◆ tapestry needle for weaving in ends

◆ stitch markers

◆ stitch holders or waste yarn

GAUGE

Stockinette stitch on US 4 (3.5 mm) needles: 20 sts and 30 rows/rounds = 4 x 5 in. (10 x 10 cm)

COLOR DESIGNATIONS

MC: Crimson

CC: Seabird

STITCH PATTERNS

Ribbing pattern in the round
Alternate "k2, p2" to end of round.

Stockinette stitch in the round
Knit all stitches in all rounds.

Stranded colorwork pattern in the round

Work all rnds in st st, following the appropriate chart.

Yoke Colorwork Chart: Repeat the pattern repeat [initially 12 sts wide] throughout the round. Work Rnds 1–28 once, increasing as stated in Rnds 5, 10, 16, 20, 22, and 26.

Sleeve Colorwork Chart: Repeat the pattern repeat [18 sts wide] throughout the round. Work Rnds 1–41 once.

PLEASE NOTE: Lock in floats after every 3rd stitch. Keep CC at the base of the finger, i.e., in front.

TIP

First, read through all the instructions and mark all numbers pertaining to the size you want to knit. This way, you are prepared in advance and don't have to search for the correct numbers while knitting.

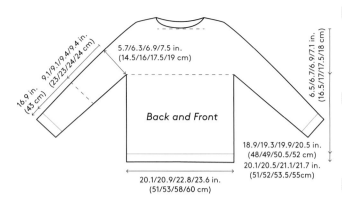

5.7/6.3/6.9/7.5 in.
(14.5/16/17.5/19 cm)

9.1/9.1/9.4/9.4 in.
(23/23/24/24 cm)

16.9 in.
(43 cm)

Back and Front

6.5/6.7/6.9/7.1 in.
(16.5/17/17.5/18 cm)

18.9/19.3/19.9/20.5 in.
(48/49/50.5/52 cm)

20.1/20.5/21.1/21.7 in.
(51/52/53.5/55cm)

20.1/20.9/22.8/23.6 in.
(51/53/58/60 cm)

INSTRUCTIONS

Using circular needle size US 2.5 (3.0 mm) and MC, CO 92/92/96/96. Join in the round, placing a marker for the BoR. Work 8 rnds in ribbing pattern.

Change to circular needle size US 4 (3.5 mm). Knit 1 rnd.

Work short rows as follows:

Row 1 (RS): Beginning at the BoR (center back), k20/20/24/24, turn work.

Row 2 (WS): DSt, purl to center back, p20/20/24/24, turn work.

Row 3 (RS): DSt, knit to center back, [k3, M1L] 5 times, k to DSt, knitting both legs of the DSt as one when you encounter it, k2, turn work.

Row 4 (WS): DSt, purl to center back, [p3, M1R] 5 times, purl to DSt, purling both legs of the DSt as one when you encounter it, p2, turn work.

Row 5 (RS): DSt, knit to center back, then continue to knit to DSt, knitting both legs of the DSt as one when you encounter it, k1, turn work.

Row 6 (WS): DSt, purl to center back, then continue p to DSt, purling both legs of the DSt as one when you encounter it, p1, turn work.

Repeat the last two rows (Rows 5 and 6) once.

Next Row (RS): DSt, knit to center back (= 102/102/106/106 sts).

Knit 1 rnd, while knitting both legs of the DSt as one.

Begin increases as follows:

Size S:

Inc Rnd 1: *K2, M1L, rep from * to end of rnd (= 153 sts).

Work 3 rnds in st st, at the same time increasing 3 sts evenly distributed throughout the last round (= 156 sts).

Size M:

Inc Rnd 1: K6, M1L, [k10, M1L] 9 times, k6 (= 112 sts).

Work 2 rnds in st st.

Inc Rnd 2: *K2, M1L, rep from * to end of rnd (= 168 sts).

Size L:

Inc Rnd 1: K8, M1L, [k7, M1L] 13 times, k7 (= 120 sts).

Work 3 rnds in st st.

Inc Rnd 2: *K2, M1L, rep from * to end of rnd (= 180 sts).

Size XL:

Inc Rnd 1: K1, M1L, [k5, M1L] 21 times (= 128 sts).

Work 3 rnds in st st.

Inc Rnd 2: *K2, M1L, rep from * to end of rnd (= 192 sts).

All Sizes:

Change to short circular needle size US 6 (4.0 mm).

Work the stranded colorwork pattern from Yoke Colorwork Chart. Repeat the pattern repeat [initially 12 sts wide] throughout the round. Work Rnds 1–28 once, increasing in Rnds 5, 10, 16, 20, 22, and 26 as stated. After Rnd 26, in each rnd, 13/14/15/16 pattern repeats [each 21 sts wide] will be worked (= 273/294/315/336 sts).

After the last rnd (= Rnd 28) in stranded colorwork pattern, break the working yarn in CC, and continue in MC only, changing to circular needle US 4 (3.5 mm).

At overall height of 6.5/6.7/6.9/7.1 in. (16.5/17/17.5/18 cm) from cast-on center front, begin short-row shaping as follows:

Row 1 (RS): Beginning at the BoR (center back), k90/94/98/102, turn work.

Row 2 (WS): DSt, purl to center back, purl an additional 90/94/98/102 sts, turn work.

Row 3 (RS): DSt, knit to 4 sts after the last DSt, knitting both legs of the DSt together as one, turn work.

Row 4 (WS): DSt, knit to 4 sts after the last DSt, purling both legs of the DSt together as one, turn work.

Rep the last two rows (Rows 3 and 4) once, for a total of 3 DSts worked on each side.

Knit 1 rnd, while knitting both legs of the DSt as one.

Divide sts for Body and Sleeves as follows:

Starting at center back, k45/47/50/53 Back sts, place 46/52/56/62 Sleeve sts on holder, CO 4/4/5/5 new sts, place m (= new BoR), CO 4/4/5/5 new sts, k90/95/102/106 Front sts, place 46/52/56/62 Sleeve sts on holder, CO 8/8/10/10 new sts, k46/48/51/53 Back sts to center back.

You now have 46/52/56/62 sts + 8/8/10/10 sts = 54/60/66/72 sts for each Sleeve, 90/95/102/106 sts for the Front, 91/95/101/106 sts + 16/16/20/20 sts for the Back = 197/206/223/232 total Body sts on the needles.

Change to circular needle size US 4 (3.5 mm), and continue in MC in st st, working until Body measures 12.4/12.6/13.2/13.4 in. (31.5/32/33.5/34 cm) from Sleeve. Change to circular needle size US 2.5 (3.0 mm) and work 8 rnds in ribbing pattern. Bind off all sts using elastic BO method.

SLEEVES (MAKE 2)

PLEASE NOTE: To avoid unsightly holes, 1 additional (unlisted) stitch should be picked up at each side of the armhole. In the following round, knit each of the 2 extra sts together with the corresponding Sleeve st to return to the original stitch count.

Take up the formerly held 46/52/56/62 Sleeve sts with DPN set size US 4 (3.5 mm), and continue in MC in st st: For the armhole, beginning at the center of the additionally CO sts of the Body, work 4/4/5/5 sts (+ 1 additionally picked up st for hole prevention, as noted) for the Sleeve into the corresponding sts at the Body; knit the Sleeve sts; into the corresponding additionally CO sts at the Body, work 4/4/5/5 sts (+ 1 additionally picked up st for hole prevention) for the Sleeve, place m (= BoR); in the following round, knit the 2 extra sts together with the adjoining sts as described above (= 54/60/66/72 sts).

Continue working st st in the round in MC until the Sleeve measures 3.1 in. (8 cm) from begin of Sleeve.

Work Dec Rnd 1 as follows: k2, k2tog, knit to 4 sts before m, skp, k2 (= 2 sts decreased = 52/58/64/70 sts).

Repeat decreases in every 14th rnd 1/2/3/4 time(s) (= 50/54/58/62 sts).

AT THE SAME TIME, when piece has reached a length of 9/9/9.5/9.5 in. (23/23/24/24 cm) from CO edge of Sleeve, using DPN set size US 6 (4.0 mm), begin stranded colorwork pattern from Sleeve Colorwork Chart. Repeat the pattern repeat [initially 18 sts wide] throughout the round. Work Rnds 1–41 once. Decreases take place at the same time; as stitch count becomes smaller, there will be an incomplete pattern repeat at the end of the rnd. (**PLEASE NOTE:** Only for size M, 3 complete pattern repeats will be worked; for all other sizes, fewer or more sts, respectively, will be worked.)

After having completed the colorwork pattern, continue in st st in the round, working until Sleeve measures approx. 15.7 in. (40 cm). For the ribbing pattern, the stitch count has to be a multiple of 4; for this rea-

son, for all sizes, the stitch count has to be adjusted by working an additional dec rnd, i.e., dec 2 sts (= 48/52/56/60 sts). Change to DPN set size US 2.5 (3.0 mm) and work 8 rnds in ribbing pattern.

Bind off all sts using elastic BO method.

FINISHING

Neatly weave in all ends. Turn the garment inside out, gently pin it into shape on an even horizontal surface, cover it with a moistened cloth, and let it dry.

SLEEVE COLORWORK CHART

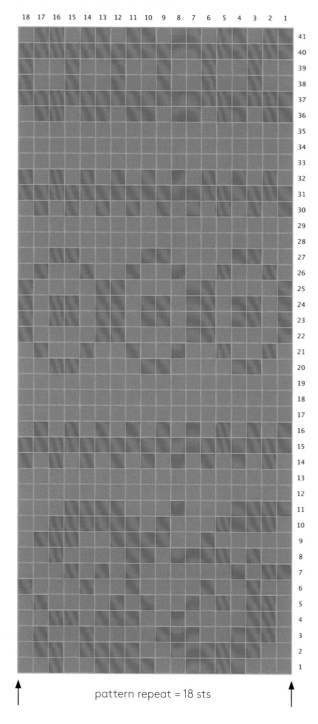

pattern repeat = 18 sts

LEGEND

= MC: Crimson

= CC: Seabird

= M1L

YOKE COLORWORK CHART

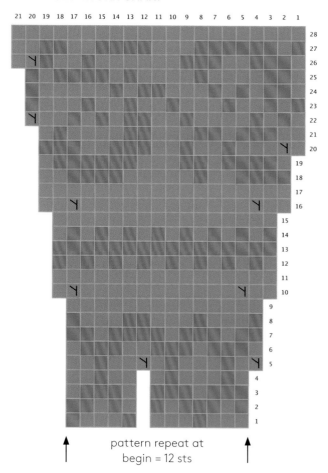

pattern repeat at
begin = 12 sts

LÁRUS

Sweater in a stranded colorwork pattern

◆◆◇

Loose Fit
Shown in size XL

SIZES

S, M, L, XL

Positive ease of at least 7.1 in. (18 cm) has already been incorporated.

PLEASE NOTE: Numbers for individual sizes are listed in order from smallest to largest size, divided by slashes. If only one number is given, it applies to all sizes.

Chest circumference: 42.1/45.7/48.8/51.2 in. (107/116/124/130 cm)

Sleeve width: 6.7/6.9/7.1/7.3 in. (17/17.5/18/18.5 cm)

MATERIALS

◆ Rauwerk Merino Sportweight; #2 fine weight; 100% merino wool; 328 yd. (300 m) per 3.5 oz. (100 g); 4/4/5/5 skeins Graphit (Gray) and 1 skein each Obsidian (Dark Gray) and Quarz (Light Gray)

PLEASE NOTE: Check the ball bands, and only use skeins of the same dye lot together. Actual total yardage may vary, depending on individual knitting style.

◆ 2 circular needles size US 2.5 (3.0 mm), 16 in. (40 cm) and 32 in. (80 cm) long

◆ 2 circular needles size US 4 (3.5 mm), 24 in. (60 cm) and 32 in. (80 cm) long

◆ 2 circular needles size US 6 (4.0 mm), 24 in. (60 cm) and 32 in. (80 cm) long

◆ DPN sets in sizes US 2.5 (3.0 mm) and US 4 (3.5 mm)

◆ tapestry needle for weaving in ends

◆ stitch markers

◆ stitch holders or waste yarn

GAUGE

Stockinette stitch in one color on US 4 (3.5 mm) needles: 19 sts and 30 rows/rounds = 4 x 4 in. (10 x 10 cm)

PLEASE NOTE: Since everybody knits differently, the stranded colorwork pattern should be swatched to determine whether a smaller or larger needle size might

be required to match the listed gauge. Needle size US 6 (4.0 mm) is recommended.

COLOR DESIGNATIONS

MC: Gray

CC1: Dark Gray

CC2: Light Gray

STITCH PATTERNS

Ribbing pattern in the round

Alternate "k2, p2" to end of round.

Stockinette stitch in the round

Knit all stitches in all rounds.

Stranded colorwork pattern in the round

Work all rnds in st st, following the appropriate chart. Repeat the pattern repeat throughout the round.

Colorwork Chart 1: Repeat the pattern repeat [6 sts wide] throughout the round. Work Rnds 1–5 once.

Colorwork Chart 2: Repeat the pattern repeat [initially 8 sts wide] throughout the round. Work Rounds 1–6 once. In Rnd 5, increase as shown.

Colorwork Chart 3: Repeat the pattern repeat [initially 15 sts wide] throughout the round. Work Rounds 1–31 once. In Rnds 3, 8, and 13, increase as shown.

PLEASE NOTE: Lock in floats after every 3rd stitch. Keep CC at the base of the finger, i.e., in front.

TIP

First, read through all the instructions and mark all numbers pertaining to the size you want to knit. This way, you are prepared in advance and don't have to search for the correct numbers while knitting.

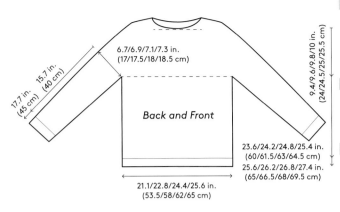

Back and Front

17.7 in. (45 cm)
15.7 in. (40 cm)
6.7/6.9/7.1/7.3 in. (17/17.5/18/18.5 cm)
9.4/9.6/9.8/10 in. (24/24.5/25/25.5 cm)
23.6/24.2/24.8/25.4 in. (60/61.5/63/64.5 cm)
25.6/26.2/26.8/27.4 in. (65/66.5/68/69.5 cm)
21.1/22.8/24.4/25.6 in. (53.5/58/62/65 cm)

INSTRUCTIONS

Using shorter circular needle in size US 2.5 (3.0 mm) and CC1, CO 88/88/92/92 sts. Join in the round and place a marker for the BoR (middle of the Back). Work 12 rnds in ribbing pattern.

Change to short circular needle size US 4 (3.5 mm). Continue working in CC1.

Work the first inc rnd for all sizes as follows:

Inc Rnd 1: *K2, M1L, rep from * to end of rnd (= 132/132/138/138 sts).

Work short rows as follows:

Row 1 (RS): Beginning at the BoR (center back), k44/46/48/50, turn work.

Row 2 (WS): DSt, purl to center back, purl an additional 44/46/48/50 sts, turn work.

Row 3 (RS): DSt, knit to 3 sts after the last DSt, knitting both legs of the DSt as one when you encounter it, turn work.

Row 4 (WS): DSt, purl to 3 sts after the last DSt, purling both legs of the DSt as one when you encounter it, turn work.

Rep the last two rows (Rows 3 and 4) once, for a total of 3 DSts worked on each side.

Knit for 2 rnds, working both legs of the DSt as one in the first rnd.

Change to short circular needle size US 6 (4.0 mm).

Work the stranded colorwork pattern from Colorwork Chart 1. Work the pattern repeat [6 sts wide] 22/22/23/23 times per round (= 132/132/138/138 sts).

Now, work Inc Rnds 2 and 3 in CC2 (Light Gray) as follows:

Size S:

Inc Rnd 2: *K3, M1L, rep from * to end of rnd (= 176 sts).

Inc Rnd 3: *K11, M1L, rep from * to end of rnd (= 192 sts).

Size M:

Inc Rnd 2: *K2, M1L, rep from * to end of rnd (= 198 sts).

Inc Rnd 3: K4, [k19, M1L] 10 times, k4 (= 208 sts).

Size L:

Inc Rnd 2: *K3, M1L, rep from * to end of rnd (= 184 sts).

Inc Rnd 3: *K6, [k4, M1L] 20 times, k6, rep from * once (= 224 sts).

Size XL:

Inc Rnd 2: *K2, M1L, rep from * to end of rnd (= 207 sts).

Inc Rnd 3: K4, [k6, M1L] 33 times, k5 (= 240 sts).

All Sizes:

Work the stranded colorwork pattern from Colorwork Chart 2. Work the pattern repeat [initially 8 sts wide] 24/26/28/30 times per round (= 192/208/224/240 sts). Work Rounds 1–6 once, working increases in Rnd 5 as shown. After this, in each round, 24/26/28/30 pattern repeats [each 9 sts wide] will be worked (= 216/234/252/270 sts).

Work Inc Rnd 3 for sizes S, M, and L in MC as follows:

Size S:

Inc Rnd 3: *K24, M1L, rep from * to end of rnd (= 225 sts).

Size M:

Inc Rnd 3: *K39, M1L, rep from * to end of rnd (= 240 sts).

Size L:

Inc Rnd 3: *K84, M1L, rep from * to end of rnd (= 255 sts).

Size XL (no increases):

Work 1 rnd even without increases (= 270 sts).

All Sizes:

Work the stranded colorwork pattern from Colorwork Chart 3. Work the pattern repeat [initially 15 sts wide] 15/16/17/18 times per round (= 225/240/255/270 sts). Work Rounds 1–31 once. In Rnds 3, 8, and 13, increase as shown. After Rnd 13, each round will have 15/16/17/18 pattern repeats [20 sts wide each] (= 300/320/340/360 sts). While working increases, change to long circular needle size US 6 (4.0 mm).

After having completed the colorwork pattern, change to circular needle size US 4 (3.5 mm) and, if needed, continue in st st in MC, until an overall height of 9.5/9.7/9.8/10 in. (24/24.5/25/25.5 cm) from CO center front has been reached. Then divide sts for Body and Sleeves as follows:

Starting at center back, k47/51/55/59 Back sts, place 56/58/60/62 Sleeve sts on holder, CO 5 new sts, place m (= new BoR), CO 5 new sts, k94/102/110/118 Front sts, place 56/58/60/62 Sleeve sts on holder, CO 10 new underarm sts, k47/51/55/59 Back sts to center back.

You now have 56/58/60/62 sts + 10 sts for each Sleeve. Front and Back each have 94/102/110/118 sts + 20 sts = 208/224/240/256 total Body sts on the needles.

Continue with circular needle size US 4 (3.5 mm) in MC in st st, working until Body measures 14.2/14.6/15/15.4 in. (36/37/38/39 cm) from Sleeve. Now, change to long circular needle size US 2.5 (3.0 mm) and work in ribbing pattern for 2 in. (5 cm). Bind off all sts using elastic BO method.

SLEEVES (MAKE 2)

PLEASE NOTE: To avoid unsightly holes, 1 additional (unlisted) stitch should be picked up at each side of the armhole. In the following round, knit each of the 2 extra sts together with the corresponding Sleeve st to return to the original stitch count.

Take up the formerly held 56/58/60/62 Sleeve sts with DPN set size US 4 (3.5 mm), and continue in MC in st st: For the armhole, beginning at the center of the additionally CO sts of the Body, work 5 sts (+ 1 additionally picked up st for hole prevention, as noted) for the Sleeve into the corresponding sts at the Body; knit the Sleeve sts; into the corresponding additionally CO sts at the Body, work 5 sts (+ 1 additionally picked up st for hole prevention) for the Sleeve, place m (= BoR); in the following round, knit the 2 extra sts together with the adjoining sts as described above (= 66/68/70/72 sts).

When piece has reached 3.2 in. (8 cm) from begin of Sleeve, work first round of sleeve tapering decreases as follows: k2, k2tog, knit to 4 sts before m, skp, k2 (= 2 sts decreased = 64/66/68/70 sts).

Repeat decreases in every 11th/10th/11th/10th rnd a total of 7/8/7/8 times (= 50/50/54/54 sts).

Continue in st st in the round, working until Sleeve either measures approx. 15.7 in. (40 cm) or is 2 in. (5 cm) shorter than desired length. Change to DPN set size US 2.5 (3.0 mm), and work ribbing pattern in MC for 2 in. (5 cm). Bind off all sts using elastic BO method.

FINISHING

Neatly weave in all ends. Turn the garment inside out, gently pin it into shape on an even horizontal surface, cover it with a moistened cloth, and let it dry.

COLORWORK CHART 1

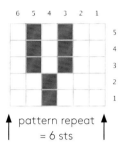

pattern repeat
= 6 sts

COLORWORK CHART 2

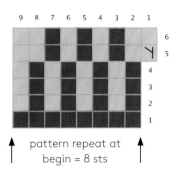

pattern repeat at
begin = 8 sts

COLORWORK CHART 3

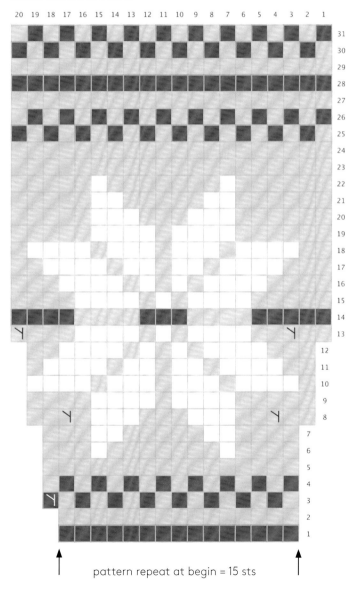

pattern repeat at begin = 15 sts

LEGEND

= MC: Gray

= CC1: Dark Gray

= CC2: Light Gray

= M1L

SÓLEY
Sweater in a stranded colorwork pattern

SIZES

S, M, L, XL

Positive ease of approx. 5.5 in. (14 cm) has already been incorporated.

PLEASE NOTE: Numbers for individual sizes are listed in order from smallest to largest size, divided by slashes. If only one number is given, it applies to all sizes.

Chest circumference: 40/42.1/45.3/47.6 in. (101/107/115/121 cm)

Sleeve width: 5.9/6.5/6.7/7.1 in. (15, 16.5, 17, 18 cm)

MATERIALS

◆ Lana Grossa Bingo; #4 medium weight; 100% pure new wool; 88 yd. (80 m) per 1.75 oz. (50 g); 11/12/13/14 skeins #24 Schwarz (Black) and 1 skein each #726 Purpurrot (Crimson Red), #05 Rohweiß (Natural White), #727 Blaupetrol (Blue Petrol), and #728 Kiwigrün (Kiwi Green)

PLEASE NOTE: Check the ball bands, and only use skeins of the same dye lot together. Actual total yardage may vary, depending on individual knitting style.

◆ 2 circular needles size US 6 (4.0 mm), 16 in. (40 cm) and 24 in. (60 cm) long

◆ 2 circular needles size US 10 (6.0 mm), 24 in. (60 cm) and 32 in. (80 cm) long

◆ DPN sets in sizes US 4 (3.5 mm), US 6 (4.0 mm), and US 10 (6.0 mm)

◆ tapestry needle for weaving in ends

◆ stitch markers

◆ stitch holders or waste yarn

GAUGE

Stockinette stitch in one color and size US 6 (4.0 mm) needles: 16 sts and 22 rows/rounds = 4 x 4 in. (10 x 10 cm)

PLEASE NOTE: Since everybody knits differently, the stranded colorwork pattern should be swatched to determine whether a smaller or larger needle size might be required to match the listed gauge. Needle size US 10 (6.0 mm) is recommended.

COLOR DESIGNATIONS

MC: Black

CC1: Crimson Red

CC2: Natural White

CC3: Blue Petrol

CC4: Kiwi Green

STITCH PATTERNS

Ribbing pattern in the round

Alternate "k2, p2" to end of round.

Stockinette stitch in the round

Knit all stitches in all rounds.

Yoke pattern in the round

Work all rnds in st st according to the colorwork chart. Repeat the pattern repeat [initially 10 sts wide] throughout the round. Work Rnds 1–33 once (according to instructions). In Rnds 5, 10, 16, and 26, increase as shown.

PLEASE NOTE: Lock in floats after every 3rd stitch. Keep CC at the base of the finger, i.e., in front.

TIP

First, read through all the instructions and mark all numbers pertaining to the size you want to knit. This way, you are prepared in advance and don't have to search for the correct numbers while knitting.

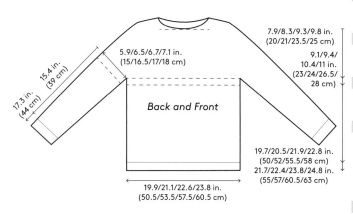

Back and Front

5.9/6.5/6.7/7.1 in. (15/16.5/17/18 cm)

15.4 in. (39 cm)

17.3 in. (44 cm)

7.9/8.3/9.3/9.8 in. (20/21/23.5/25 cm)

9.1/9.4/10.4/11 in. (23/24/26.5/28 cm)

19.7/20.5/21.9/22.8 in. (50/52/55.5/58 cm)

21.7/22.4/23.8/24.8 in. (55/57/60.5/63 cm)

19.9/21.1/22.6/23.8 in. (50.5/53.5/57.5/60.5 cm)

INSTRUCTIONS

Using DPN set in size US 6 (4.0 mm) and MC, CO 64/64/68/68 sts. Join in the round and place a marker for the BoR (middle of the Back). Work 6 rnds in ribbing pattern.

Change to short circular needle size US 6 (4.0 mm). Work as follows, beginning with increases:

Sizes S and M:

Inc Rnd 1: *K2, M1L, rep from * to end of rnd (= 96 sts).

Work 3 rnds in st st.

Sizes L and XL:

Inc Rnd 1: *K2, M1L, rep from * to end of rnd (= 102 sts).

Work 1 rnd in st st.

Inc Rnd 2: K1, M1L, [k4, M1L] 25 times, k1 (= 128 sts).

All Sizes:

Work short rows as follows:

Row 1 (RS): Beginning at the BoR (center back), k32/34/36/38, turn work.

Row 2 (WS): DSt, purl to center back, purl an additional 32/34/36/38 sts, turn work.

Row 3 (RS): DSt, knit to 3 sts after the last DSt, knitting both legs of the DSt as one when you encounter it, turn work.

Row 4 (WS): DSt, purl to 3 sts after the last DSt, purling both legs of the DSt as one when you encounter it, turn work.

Rep the last two rows (Rows 3 and 4) once, for a total of 3 DSts worked on each side.

Then, knit for 2 rnds, working both legs of the DSt as one in Rnd 1.

Now, work Inc Rnds as follows:

Size S:

Inc Rnd 2: M1L, [k3, M1L] 32 times, M1L (= 130 sts).

Size M:

Inc Rnd 2: K4, [k2, M1L] 44 times, k4 (= 140 sts).

Size L:

Inc Rnd 3: K1, M1L, [k6, M1L] 21 times, k1 (= 150 sts).

Size XL:

Inc Rnd 3: *K4, M1L, rep from * to end of rnd (= 160 sts).

Change to short circular needle size US 10 (6.0 mm).

All Sizes:

Work Yoke Pattern from colorwork chart. Work the pattern repeat [initially 10 sts wide] 13/14/15/16 times per round (= 130/140/150/160 sts). Work Rnds 1–33 once. In Rnds 5, 10, 16, and 26, increase as shown. After Rnd 26, 13/14/15/16 pattern repeats [each 18 sts wide] will be worked per round (= 234/252/270/288 sts). If needed, change to longer circular needle size US 10 (6.0 mm) to accommodate the larger stitch count. AT THE SAME TIME, when piece has reached a height of 7.9/8.3/9.3/9.8 in. (20/21/23.5/25 cm) from CO center front, divide sts for Body and Sleeves as follows:

Starting at center back, k37/40/43/46 Back sts, place 42/46/49/52 Sleeve sts on holder, CO 3 new sts (continuing to follow the Yoke Pattern), place m (= new BoR), CO 3 new sts (continuing to follow the Yoke Pattern), k75/80/86/92 Front sts, place 42/46/49/52 Sleeve sts on holder, CO 6 new sts (continuing to follow the Yoke Pattern), k38/40/43/46 Back sts to center back.

You now have 42/46/49/52 sts + 6 sts = 48/52/55/58 sts for each Sleeve. Front and Back each have 75/80/86/92 sts + 12 sts = 162/172/184/196 total Body sts on the needles.

Change to short circular needle size US 10 (6.0 mm). Using MC and CC4, work another 1.2 in. (3 cm) in Yoke Pattern, then break CC4. Change to US 6 (4.0 mm) needles, and continue in MC in st st, working until Body measures 11.8/12.2/12.6/13 in. (30/31/32/33 cm) from Sleeve. Then, change to long circular needle size US 4 (3.5 mm), and work in ribbing pattern for 2 in. (5 cm). Bind off all sts using elastic BO method.

SLEEVES (MAKE 2)

PLEASE NOTE: To avoid unsightly holes, pick up 1 additional (unlisted) st at each side of the armhole, using the same color as the adjoining Sleeve st. Pick up new sts alternatingly in MC and CC4 in Yoke Pattern. In the following round, knit each of the 2 extra sts together with the corresponding Sleeve st to return to the original stitch count.

Take up the formerly held 42/46/49/52 Sleeve sts with DPN set size US 10 (6.0 mm), and continue in MC and CC4 in Yoke Pattern: For the armhole, beginning at the center of the additionally CO sts of the Body, work 3 sts (+ 1 additionally picked up st for hole prevention, as noted) for the Sleeve into the corresponding sts at the Body; knit the Sleeve sts; into the corresponding additionally CO sts at the Body, work 3 sts (+ 1 additionally picked up st for hole prevention) for the sleeve, place m (= BoR); in the following round, knit the 2 extra sts together with the adjoining sts as described above (= 48/52/55/58 sts); at the same time in Rnd 1 adjusting the stitch count for size L by increasing 1 st, and for size XL by increasing 2 sts evenly distributed (= 48/52/56/60 sts).

Now, continue in Yoke Pattern, working in MC and CC4, until the Sleeve yoke has reached the same height as the Body yoke, then break CC4.

Change to DPN set size US 6 (4.0 mm), and continue in MC in st st.

When piece has reached 3.2 in. (8 cm) from begin of Sleeve, work first round of sleeve tapering decreases as follows: k2, k2tog, knit to 4 sts before m, skp, k2 (= 2 sts decreased = 46/50/54/58 sts).

Repeat decreases in every 22nd/13th/13th/9th round a total of 3/5/5/7 times (= 40/40/44/44 sts).

Continue in st st in the round, working until Sleeve either measures approx. 15.4 in. (39 cm) or is 2 in. (5 cm) shorter than desired length. Now, change to DPN set size US 4 (3.5 mm) and work ribbing pattern in MC for 2 in. (5 cm). Bind off all sts using elastic BO method.

FINISHING

Neatly weave in all ends. Turn the garment inside out, gently pin it into shape on an even horizontal surface, cover it with a moistened cloth, and let it dry.

YOKE COLORWORK CHART

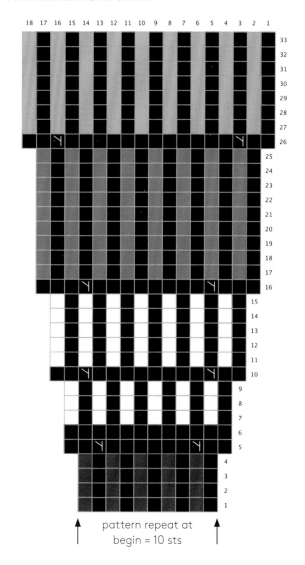

pattern repeat at begin = 10 sts

LEGEND

= MC: Black

= CC1: Crimson Red

= CC2: Natural White

= CC3: Blue Petrol

= CC4: Kiwi Green

= M1L

VALA
Sweater with cable pattern

◆◆◆

Regular Fit
Shown in size S

SIZES

S, M, L, XL

Positive ease of approx. 5.5 in. (14 cm) has already been incorporated.

PLEASE NOTE: Numbers for individual sizes are listed in order from smallest to largest size, divided by slashes. If only one number is given, it applies to all sizes.

Chest circumference: 40.2/43.3/46.5/49.2 in. (102/110/118/125 cm)

Sleeve width: 6.1/6.3/6.7/6.9 in. (15.5/16/17/17.5 cm)

MATERIALS

◆ Isager Silk Mohair; #0 lace weight; 75% super kid mohair, 25% silk; 232 yd. (212 m) per 0.9 oz. (25 g); 3/3/4/5 skeins #6 Nude and 1 skein #7 Braun (Brown)

PLEASE NOTE: Check the ball bands, and only use skeins of the same dye lot together. Actual total yardage may vary, depending on individual knitting style.

◆ 2 circular needles size US 7 (4.5 mm), 16 in. (40 cm) and 32 in. (80 cm) long

◆ DPN set size US 7 (4.5 mm)

◆ cable needle or auxiliary needle

◆ tapestry needle for weaving in ends

◆ stitch markers

◆ stitch holders or waste yarn

GAUGE

In Cable Pattern on US 7 (4.5 mm) needles: 16 sts and 26 rows/rounds = 4 x 4 in. (10 x 10 cm)

COLOR DESIGNATIONS

MC: Nude

CC: Brown

STITCH PATTERNS

Stockinette stitch in the round

Knit all stitches in all rounds.

Cable pattern

Work all rnds from the appropriate chart.

Knitting Chart 1: Repeat the pattern repeat [20 sts wide] throughout the round. Work Rnds 1–12 once, increasing in Rnd 12 as shown.

Knitting Chart 2: Repeat the pattern repeat [initially 24 sts wide] throughout the round. Repeat Rnds 1–6 as stated in the instructions, working increases in Rnd 6 (= every pattern repeat adds 4 sts). The stitch count in the stockinette sections between the cables increases accordingly (not shown in the chart).

TIP

First, read through all the instructions and mark all numbers pertaining to the size you want to knit. This way, you are prepared in advance and don't have to search for the correct numbers while knitting.

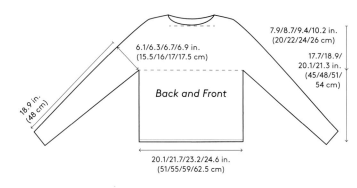

6.1/6.3/6.7/6.9 in.
(15.5/16/17/17.5 cm)

7.9/8.7/9.4/10.2 in.
(20/22/24/26 cm)

17.7/18.9/20.1/21.3 in.
(45/48/51/54 cm)

18.9 in.
(48 cm)

Back and Front

20.1/21.7/23.2/24.6 in.
(51/55/59/62.5 cm)

INSTRUCTIONS

Using shorter circular needle size US 7 (4.5 mm) and MC, CO 80/80/100/100 sts. Join in the round and place a marker for the BoR (middle of the Back).

Work in Cable pattern from Knitting Chart 1. Work the pattern repeat [20 sts wide] 4/4/5/5 times per round. Work Rnds 1–12 once, increasing in Rnd 12 as shown (= 96/96/120/120 sts).

Now, continue in Cable pattern from Knitting Chart 2. Work the pattern repeat [initially 24 sts wide] 4/4/5/5 times per round. Repeat Rnds 1–6 all the time, working increases in Rnd 6 (= every pattern repeat adds 4 sts). The stitch count in the stockinette sections between the cables increases accordingly (4 sts/6 sts/8 sts/10 sts, etc.).

AT THE SAME TIME, during the first heightwise repeat of the Cable pattern, in Rnd 3 of Knitting Chart 2, work short rows as follows, staying in cable pattern:

Row 1 (RS): Beginning at the BoR (center back), k27/27/36/36, turn work.

Row 2 (WS): DSt, purl to center back, purl an additional 27/27/36/36 sts, turn work.

Row 3 (RS): DSt, work to 3 sts before the last DSt, turn work.

Row 4 (WS): DSt, work to 3 sts before the last DSt, turn work.

Rep the last two rows (Rows 3 and 4) once, for a total of 3 DSts worked on each side.

Then, knit 1 rnd, knitting both legs of the DSt as one when you encounter it.

Work Rnds 1–6 of the Cable pattern from Knitting Chart 2 a total of 9/10/11/12 times (= 240/256/272/288 sts).

AT THE SAME TIME, at overall height of 7.9/8.7/9.5/10.2 in. (20/22/24/26 cm) from cast-on, again in a Rnd 3 of a heightwise repeat, work short-row shaping as follows:

Row 1 (RS): Beginning at the BoR (center back), k80/84/88/92, turn work.

Row 2 (WS): DSt, purl to center back, purl an additional 80/84/88/92 sts, turn work.

Row 3 (RS): DSt, knit to 5 sts after the last DSt, knitting both legs of the DSt together as one. Turn work.

Row 4 (WS): DSt, purl to 5 sts after the last DSt, purling both legs of the DSt together as one. Turn work.

Rep the last two rows (Rows 3 and 4) once, for a total of 3 DSts worked on each side.

Then, knit 1 rnd, knitting both legs of the DSt as one when you encounter it.

In the following round, divide sts for Body and Sleeves as follows:

Starting at center back, k38/41/44/47 Back sts, place 44/46/48/50 Sleeve sts on holder, CO 3 new sts, place m (= new BoR), CO 3 new sts, k76/82/88/94 Front sts, place 44/46/48/50 Sleeve sts on holder, CO 6 new sts, k38/41/44/47 Back sts to center back.

You now have 44/46/48/50 sts + 6 sts = 50/52/54/56 sts for each Sleeve. Front and Back each have 76/82/88/94 sts + 12 sts = 164/176/188/200 total Body sts on the needles.

Continue in Cable pattern (working the newly added sts in st st), until Body measures 9.5/9.8/10.2/10.7 in. (24/25/26/27 cm) from Sleeve. Change to CC and work 4 rnds in st st. Bind off all sts using elastic BO method.

SLEEVES (MAKE 2)

PLEASE NOTE: To avoid unsightly holes, 1 additional (unlisted) st should be picked up at each side of the armhole. In the following round, knit each of the 2 extra sts together with the corresponding Sleeve st to return to the original stitch count.

Take up the formerly held 44/46/48/50 Sleeve sts with a size US 7 (4.5 mm) DPN set: For the armhole, beginning at the center of the additionally CO sts of the Body, work 3 sts (+ 1 additionally picked up st for hole prevention, as noted) for the Sleeve into the corresponding sts at the Body; knit the Sleeve sts; into the corresponding additionally CO sts at the Body, work 3 sts (+ 1 additionally picked up st for hole prevention) for the Sleeve, place m (= BoR); in the following round, knit the 2 extra sts together with the adjoining sts as described above (= 50/52/54/56 sts).

Continue in st st. When piece has reached 3.2 in. (8 cm) from begin of Sleeve, work first sleeve tapering dec rnd as follows: k2, k2tog, knit to 4 sts before m, skp, k2 (= 48/50/52/54 sts).

Repeat decreases in every 16th rnd 6 times more
(= 36/38/40/42 sts).

Continue in st st in the round, working until Sleeve either
measures approx. 19 in. (48 cm) or has reached other
desired length. Bind off all sts using elastic BO method.

FINISHING

Neatly weave in all ends. Turn the garment inside out,
gently pin it into shape on an even horizontal surface,
cover it with a moistened cloth, and let it dry.

KNITTING CHART 1

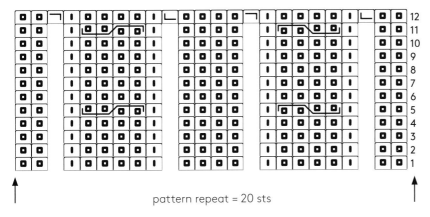

pattern repeat = 20 sts

KNITTING CHART 2

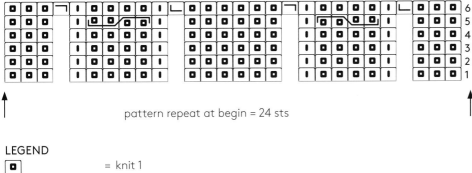

pattern repeat at begin = 24 sts

LEGEND

▢	= knit 1
▮	= purl 1
	= cable 4 sts to the left: hold 2 sts on cable needle in front of work, k2, then knit the sts from the cable needle
	= cable 4 sts to the right: hold 2 sts on cable needle behind work, k2, then knit the sts from the cable needle
¬	= M1L
L	= M1R

ÁSTHILDUR
Sweater in a stranded colorwork pattern

◆◆◆

SIZES

S, M, L, XL

Positive ease of up to 2.4 in. (6 cm) has been incorporated.

PLEASE NOTE: Numbers for individual sizes are listed in order from smallest to largest size, divided by slashes. If only one number is given, it applies to all sizes.

Chest circumference: 35.8/40.2/42.5/45 in. (91/102/108/114 cm)

Sleeve width: 5.5/6.1/6.3/6.5 in. (14/15.5/16/16.5 cm)

MATERIALS

◆ Lana Grossa Alta Moda Alpaca; #4 medium weight; 90% alpaca, 5% pure new wool, 5% polyamide; 153 yd. (140 m) per 1.75 oz. (50 g); 7/8/9/10 skeins #20 Brombeer/Grau Meliert (Blackberry/Gray Heathered) and 1 skein each #14 Rohweiß (Natural White) and #15 Grau/Beige Meliert (Gray/Beige Heathered)

PLEASE NOTE: Check the ball bands, and only use skeins of the same dye lot together. Actual total yardage may vary, depending on individual knitting style.

◆ 2 circular needles size US 6 (4.0 mm), 16 in. (40 cm) and 32 in. (80 cm) long
◆ circular needle size US 7 (4.5 mm), 24 in. (60 cm) long
◆ 2 circular needles size US 10 (6.0 mm), 24 in. (60 cm) and 32 in. (80 cm) long
◆ DPN sets sizes US 6 (4.0 mm) and US 7 (4.5 mm)
◆ tapestry needle for weaving in ends
◆ stitch markers
◆ stitch holders or waste yarn

GAUGE

Stockinette stitch in one color on US 7 (4.5 mm) needles: 20 sts and 28 rows/rounds = 4 x 4 in. (10 x 10 cm)

PLEASE NOTE: Since everybody knits differently, the stranded colorwork pattern should be swatched to determine whether a smaller or larger needle size might be required to match the listed gauge. Needle size US 10 (6.0 mm) is recommended.

COLOR DESIGNATIONS

MC: Blackberry/Gray Heathered

CC1: Natural White

CC2: Gray/Beige Heathered

STITCH PATTERNS

Ribbing pattern in the round

Alternate "k2, p2" to end of round.

Stockinette stitch in the round

Knit all stitches in all rounds.

Stranded colorwork pattern in the round

Work all rnds in st st, following the appropriate chart. Repeat the pattern repeat throughout the round.

Colorwork Chart 1: The pattern repeat is 6 sts wide. Work Rnds 1–5 once.

Colorwork Chart 2: The pattern repeat is initially 8 sts wide. Work Rounds 1–4 once. In Rnd 3, increase as shown.

Colorwork Chart 3: The pattern repeat is initially 12 sts wide. Work Rnds 1–21 once. In Rnds 7 and 13, increase as shown.

PLEASE NOTE: Lock in floats after every 3rd stitch. Keep CC at the base of the finger, i.e., in front.

TIP

First, read through all the instructions and mark all numbers pertaining to the size you want to knit. This way, you are prepared in advance and don't have to search for the correct numbers while knitting.

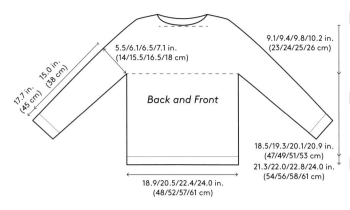

5.5/6.1/6.5/7.1 in. (14/15.5/16.5/18 cm)

9.1/9.4/9.8/10.2 in. (23/24/25/26 cm)

17.7 in. (45 cm)   15.0 in. (38 cm)

Back and Front

18.5/19.3/20.1/20.9 in. (47/49/51/53 cm)

21.3/22.0/22.8/24.0 in. (54/56/58/61 cm)

18.9/20.5/22.4/24.0 in. (48/52/57/61 cm)

INSTRUCTIONS

Using shorter circular needle size US 6 (4.0 mm) and MC, CO 96/96/100/100 sts. Join in the round and place a marker for the BoR (middle of the Back). Work 3.2 in. (8 cm) in ribbing pattern.

Now, work first inc rnd as follows:

Sizes S and M:

Inc Rnd 1: K3, [k3, M1L] 30 times, k3 (= 126 sts).

Sizes L and XL:

Inc Rnd 1: K2, [k3 M1L] 32 times, k2 (= 132 sts).

All Sizes:

Work short rows as follows:

Row 1 (RS): Beginning at the BoR (center back), k40/42/44/46, turn work.

Row 2 (WS): DSt, purl to center back, p40/42/44/46, turn work.

Row 3 (RS): DSt, knit to 3 sts after the last DSt, knitting both legs of the DSt as one when you encounter it, turn work.

Row 4 (WS): DSt, purl to 3 sts after the last DSt, purling both legs of the DSt together as one, turn work.

Rep the last two rows (Rows 3 and 4) once, for a total of 3 DSts worked on each side.

Knit for 2 rnds, working both legs of the DSt as one in the first rnd.

Work the stranded colorwork pattern from Colorwork Chart 1. Work the pattern repeat [6 sts wide] 21/21/22/22 times per round (= 126/126/132/132 sts).

Afterwards, work Inc Rnds 2 and 3 in MC as follows:

Size S:

Inc Rnd 2: K1, [k4, M1L, k1] 31 times (= 157 sts).

Inc Rnd 3: K1, [k52, M1L] 3 times (= 160 sts).

Size M:

Inc Rnd 2: *K2, M1L, rep from * to end of rnd (= 189 sts).

Inc Rnd 3: *K63, M1L, rep from * to end of rnd (= 192 sts).

Size L:

Inc Rnd 2: *K2, M1L, rep from * to end of rnd (= 198 sts).

Inc Rnd 3: K4, [k19, M1L] 10 times, k4 (= 208 sts).

Size XL:

Inc Rnd 2: *K2, M1L, rep from * to end of rnd (= 198 sts).

Inc Rnd 3: K8, [k7, M1L] 26 times, k8 (= 224 sts).

Change to short circular needle size US 10 (6.0 mm).

Work the stranded colorwork pattern from Colorwork Chart 2. Work the pattern repeat [initially 8 sts wide] 20/24/26/28 times per round. Work Rounds 1–4 once. In Rnd 3, increase as shown. In Rnd 4, 20/24/26/28 pattern repeats [each 9 sts wide] will be worked (= 180/216/234/252 sts).

Afterwards, work Inc Rnd 4 for sizes S, M, and L (size XL has no increases) in MC as follows:

Size S:

Inc Rnd 4: K6, [k7, M1L] 24 times, k6 (= 204 sts).

Size M:

Inc Rnd 4: *K18, M1L, rep from * to end of rnd (= 228 sts).

Size L:

Inc Rnd 4: *K39, M1L, rep from * to end of rnd (= 240 sts).

Size XL (no increases):

Work 1 rnd even without increases in MC.

All Sizes:

Work the stranded colorwork pattern from Colorwork Chart 3. Work the pattern repeat [initially 12 sts wide] 17/19/20/21 times per round (= 204/228/240/252 sts). Work Rnds 1–21 once. In Rnds 7 and 13, increase as shown. After Rnd 13, 17/19/20/21 pattern repeats [each 16 sts wide] will be worked (= 272/304/320/336 sts). If needed, change to longer circular needle size US 10 (6.0 mm) to accommodate the larger stitch count.

After having completed the colorwork pattern, change to circular needle size US 7 (4.5 mm) and, if needed, continue in MC in st st, working until an overall height of 8.7/9/9.8/10.7 in. (22/23/25/27 cm) from CO center front has been reached. Then, divide sts for Body and Sleeves as follows: Starting at center back,

k43/48/51/54 Back sts, place 50/56/58/60 Sleeve sts on holder, CO 3 new sts, place m (= new BoR), CO 3 new sts, k86/96/102/108 sts Front sts, place 50/56/58/60 Sleeve sts on holder, CO 6 new sts, k43/48/51/54 Back sts to center back.

You now have 50/56/58/60 sts + 6 sts = 56/62/64/66 sts for each Sleeve. Front and Back each have 86/96/102/108 sts + 12 sts = 184/204/216/228 total Body sts on the needles.

Continue with circular needle size US 7 (4.5 mm) in MC in st st, working until Body measures 12.6/13/13.4/13.8 in. (32/33/34/35 cm) from Sleeves. Now, change to long circular needle size US 6 (4.0 mm) and work in ribbing pattern for 2 in. (5 cm). Bind off all sts using elastic BO method.

SLEEVES (MAKE 2)

PLEASE NOTE: To avoid unsightly holes, 1 additional (unlisted) stitch should be picked up at each side of the armhole. In the following round, knit each of the 2 extra sts together with the corresponding Sleeve st to return to the original stitch count.

Take up the formerly held 50/56/58/60 Sleeve sts with DPN set size US 4 (3.5 mm) and continue in MC in st st: For the armhole, beginning at the center of the additionally CO sts of the Body, work 3 sts (+ 1 additionally picked up st for hole prevention, as noted) for the Sleeve into the corresponding sts at the Body; knit the Sleeve sts; into the corresponding additionally CO sts at the Body, work 3 sts (+ 1 additionally picked up st for hole prevention) for the Sleeve, place m (= BoR); in the following round, knit the 2 extra sts together with the adjoining sts as described above (= 56/62/64/66 sts).

Continue, working in MC in st st. When piece has reached 3.2 in. (8 c) from begin of Sleeve, work first sleeve tapering dec rnd as follows: k2, k2tog, knit to 4 sts before m, skp, k2 (= 2 sts decreased = 54/60/62/64 sts).

Repeat decreases in every 16th/11th/11th/9th rnd (= 44/46/48/48 sts) 5/7/7/8 times.

For size M only, adjust the stitch count for the ribbing pattern by further decreasing 2 additional sts evenly distributed (44/44/48/48 sts). Continue in st st in the round, working until Sleeve either measures approx. 16.5 in. (42 cm) or is 2.4 in. (6 cm) shorter than desired length. Change to DPN set size US 6 (4.0 mm) and work 2.4 in. (6 cm) in ribbing pattern in MC. Bind off all sts using elastic BO method.

FINISHING

Fold the collar inward and, using a strand of working yarn in MC, sew down all around in whipstitch. Neatly weave in all ends. Turn the garment inside out, gently pin it into shape on an even horizontal surface, cover it with a moistened cloth, and let it dry.

COLORWORK CHART 1

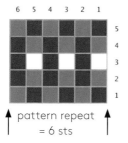

↑ pattern repeat
= 6 sts ↑

COLORWORK CHART 2

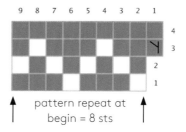

↑ pattern repeat at
begin = 8 sts ↑

COLORWORK CHART 3

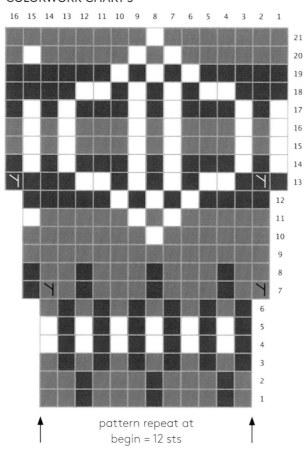

↑ pattern repeat at
begin = 12 sts ↑

LEGEND

= MC: Blackberry/Gray Heathered

= CC1: Natural White

= CC2: Gray/Beige Heathered

= M1L

SVALA
Sweater in a stripe pattern

◆◆◆

Loose Fit
Shown in size S

SIZES

S, M, L, XL

Positive ease of at least 7.1 in. (18 cm) has already been incorporated.

PLEASE NOTE: Numbers for individual sizes are listed in order from smallest to largest size, divided by slashes. If only one number is given, it applies to all sizes.

Chest circumference: 42.5/45/47.2/49.6 in. (108/114/120/126 cm)

Sleeve width: 6.5/6.9/7.3/7.5 in. (16.5/17.5/18.5/19 cm)

MATERIALS

◆ Rowan Kidsilk Haze; #0 lace weight; 70% mohair, 30% silk; 225 yd. (210 m) per 0.88 oz. (25 g); 1/2/2/2 skeins #641 Blackcurrant and #600 Dewberry), and 1 skein each #590 Pearl, #664 Steel, #612 White, #678 Purplicious, and #605 Smoke

PLEASE NOTE: Check the ball bands, and only use skeins of the same dye lot together. Actual total yardage may vary, depending on individual knitting style.

◆ circular needle size US 4 (3.5 mm), 16 in. (40 cm) long

◆ 2 circular needles size US 6 (4.0 mm), 16 in. (40 cm) and 32 in. (80 cm) long

◆ DPN sets US 6 (4.0 mm) and US 4 (3.5 mm)

◆ tapestry needle for weaving in ends

◆ stitch markers

◆ stitch holders or waste yarn

GAUGE

Stockinette stitch on US 6 (4.0 mm) needles: 14 sts and 26 rows/rounds = 4 x 4 in. (10 x 10 cm)

COLOR DESIGNATIONS

Color 1: Blackcurrant

Color 2: Dewberry

Color 3: Pearl

Color 4: Steel

Color 5: White

Color 6: Purplicious

Color 7: Smoke

STITCH PATTERNS

Ribbing pattern in the round

Alternate "k2, p2" to end of round.

Stockinette stitch in the round

Knit all stitches in all rounds.

TIP

First, read through all the instructions and mark all numbers pertaining to the size you want to knit. This way, you are prepared in advance and don't have to search for the correct numbers while knitting.

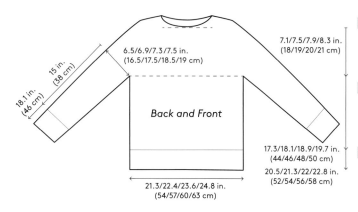

6.5/6.9/7.3/7.5 in.
(16.5/17.5/18.5/19 cm)

7.1/7.5/7.9/8.3 in.
(18/19/20/21 cm)

15 in.
(38 cm)

18.1 in.
(46 cm)

Back and Front

17.3/18.1/18.9/19.7 in.
(44/46/48/50 cm)

20.5/21.3/22/22.8 in.
(52/54/56/58 cm)

21.3/22.4/23.6/24.8 in.
(54/57/60/63 cm)

INSTRUCTIONS

Using shorter circular needle size US 4 (3.5 mm) and Color 1, CO 112/112/116/116 sts. Join in the round and place a marker for the BoR (middle of the Back). Work in ribbing pattern for 1.6 in. (4 cm).

Change to short circular needle size US 6 (4.0 mm) and Color 2, and work 1 rnd in st st.

Now, work Inc Rnd 1 as follows:

Sizes S and M:

Inc Rnd 1: K2, [k3, M1L] 36 times, k2 (= 148 sts).

Work 1 rnd in st st.

Sizes L and XL:

Inc Rnd 1: *K2, M1L, rep from * to end of rnd (= 174 sts).

All Sizes:

Work short rows as follows:

Row 1 (RS): Beginning at the BoR (center back), k46/48/50/52, turn work.

Row 2 (WS): DSt, purl to center back, purl an additional 46/48/50/52 sts, turn work.

Row 3 (RS): DSt, knit to 3 sts after the last DSt, knitting both legs of the DSt as one when you encounter it, turn work.

Row 4 (WS): DSt, purl to 3 sts after the last DSt, purling both legs of the DSt as one when you encounter it, turn work.

Rep the last two rows (Rows 3 and 4) once, for a total of 3 DSts worked on each side.

Then, knit 1 rnd, knitting both legs of the DSt as one when you encounter it.

Work 7 rnds in st st.

Then, work increases again as follows:

Size S:

Inc Rnd 2: *K4, M1L, rep from * to end of rnd (= 185 sts).

Work 1 rnd in st st.

Size M:

Inc Rnd 2: *K4, M1L, rep from * to end of rnd (= 185 sts).

Inc Rnd 3: K2, [k12, M1L] 15 times, k3 (= 200 sts).

Size L:

Inc Rnd 2: K1, [k4, M1L] 43 times, k1 (= 217 sts).

Inc Rnd 3: *K31, M1L, rep from * to end of rnd (= 224 sts).

Size XL:

Inc Rnd 2: *K3, M1L, rep from * to end of rnd (= 232 sts).

Inc Rnd 3: *K29, M1L, rep from * to end of rnd (= 240 sts).

All Sizes:

Change to long circular needle size US 6 (4.0 mm), and work stripe sequence for the yoke as follows:

In Color 2, work 12 rnds in st st.

In Color 3, work 12 rnds in st st.

In Color 4, work 1 rnd in st st.

Then, work the next set of increases in Color 4 as follows:

Size S:

Inc Rnd 3: K5, [k5, M1L] 35 times, k5 (= 220 sts).

Size M:

Inc Rnd 4: *K10, [k5, M1L] 18 times, rep from * once (= 236 sts).

Size L:

Inc Rnd 4: K4, [k9, M1L] 24 times, k4 (= 248 sts).

Size XL:

Inc Rnd 4: *K12, M1L, rep from * to end of rnd (= 260 sts).

All Sizes:

Work 10 rnds in Color 4 in st st.

Continue in Color 5 in st st. At overall height of 7.1/7.5/7.9/8.3 in. (18/19/20/21 cm) from cast-on, begin short-row shaping as follows:

Row 1 (RS): Beginning at the BoR (center back), k70/74/78/82, turn work.

Row 2 (WS): DSt, purl to center back, purl an additional 70/74/78/82 sts, turn work.

Row 3 (RS): DSt, knit to 5 sts after the last DSt, knitting both legs of the DSt together as one. Turn work.

Row 4 (WS): DSt, purl to 5 sts after the last DSt, purling both legs of the DSt together as one. Turn work.

Rep the last two rows (Rows 3 and 4) once, for a total of 3 DSts worked on each side.

Then, knit 1 rnd, knitting both legs of the DSt as one when you encounter it.

In the following round, divide sts for Body and Sleeves as follows: Starting at center back, k35/37/39/41 Back sts, place 40/44/46/48 Sleeve sts on holder, CO 3 new sts, place m (= new BoR), CO 3 new sts, k70/74/78/82 Front sts, place 40/44/46/48 Sleeve sts on holder, CO 6 new sts, k35/37/39/41 Back sts to center back.

You now have 40/44/46/48 sts + 6 sts = 46/50/52/54 sts for each Sleeve. Front and Back each have 70/74/78/82 sts + 12 sts = 152/160/168/176 total Body sts on the needles.

Work 12 rnds (from center front) in Color 5 in st st, then change to Color 6.

Work 12 rnds in Color 6 in st st.

Work 12 rnds in Color 7 in st st.

Work 6 rnds in Color 5 in st st.

Change to Color 2 and continue, working in st st, until Body measures 10.2/10.7/11/11.4 in. (26/27/28/29 cm) from Sleeve. Now, change to long circular needle size US 4 (3.5 mm) and to Color 1, and work 3.2 in. (8 cm) in ribbing pattern. When overall height from CO center front is 20.5/21.3/22/22.8 in. (52/54/56/58 cm), bind off all sts using elastic BO method.

SLEEVES (MAKE 2)

PLEASE NOTE: To avoid unsightly holes, 1 additional (unlisted) stitch should be picked up at each side of the armhole. In the following round, knit each of the 2 extra sts together with the corresponding Sleeve st to return to the original stitch count.

Take up the formerly held 40/44/46/48 Sleeve sts with a DPN set in size US 6 (4.0 mm), and work in Color 5, for the armhole, beginning at the center of the additionally CO sts of the Body, work 3 sts (+ 1 additionally picked up st for hole prevention, as noted) for the Sleeve; knit the Sleeve sts; into the corresponding additionally CO sts at the Body, work 3 sts (+ 1 additionally picked up st for hole prevention) for the Sleeve, place m (= BoR); in the following round, knit the 2 extra sts together with the adjoining sts as described above (= 46/50/52/54 sts).

Now, continue in Color 5, working until the Color 5 section at the Sleeve has reached the same height as the Color 5 section on the Body. Break Color 5 and continue, following the same stripe sequence as for the Body, but making the stripe in Color 2 about 2 in. (5 cm) longer than on the Body, until Sleeve either measures approx. 15 in. (38 cm) or is 3.1 in. (8 cm) shorter than desired length. Change to DPN set in size US 4 (3.5 mm) and work 3.1 in. (8 cm) in Color 1 in ribbing pattern. Bind off all sts using elastic BO method.

FINISHING

Neatly weave in all ends. Turn the garment inside out, gently pin it into shape on an even horizontal surface, cover it with a moistened cloth, and let it dry.

THORGEIR
Sweater in a stranded colorwork pattern

◆◆◆

Regular Fit
Shown in size M

SIZES

S, M, L, XL

Positive ease of approx. 5.5 in. (14 cm) has already been incorporated.

PLEASE NOTE: Numbers for individual sizes are listed in order from smallest to largest size, divided by slashes. If only one number is given, it applies to all sizes.

Chest circumference: 39/41.7/45/48 in. (99/106/114/122 cm)

Sleeve width: 5.9/6.3/6.7/7.1 in. (15/16/17/18 cm)

MATERIALS

◆ Lana Grossa McWool; #2 fine weight; 50% cotton, 50% acrylic; 109 yd. (100 m) per 1.75 oz. (50 g); 10/11/12/13 skeins #120 Schwarz (Black), 2 skeins #145 Grau (Gray), and 1 skein #114 Petrol

PLEASE NOTE: Check the ball bands, and only use skeins of the same dye lot together. Actual total yardage may vary, depending on individual knitting style.

◆ circular needle size US 4 (3.5 mm), 16 in. (40 cm) long

◆ circular needle size US 6 (4.0 mm), 24 in. (60 cm) long

◆ 2 circular needles size US 8 (5.0 mm), 24 in. (60 cm) and 32 in. (80 cm) long

◆ DPN sets size US 6 (4.0 mm) and US 8 (5.0 mm)

◆ tapestry needle for weaving in ends

◆ stitch markers

◆ stitch holders or waste yarn

GAUGE

Stockinette stitch in one color and size US 6 (4.0 mm) needles: 21 sts and 25 rows/rounds = 4 x 4 in. (10 x 10 cm)

PLEASE NOTE: Since everybody knits differently, the two-color stranded pattern (Colorwork Chart 1) should be swatched to determine whether a smaller or larger needle size might be required to match the listed gauge. Needle size US 8 (5.0 mm) is recommended.

COLOR DESIGNATIONS

MC: Black

CC1: Gray

CC2: Petrol

STITCH PATTERNS

Ribbing pattern in the round

Alternate "k2, p2" to end of round.

Stockinette stitch in the round

Knit all stitches in all rounds.

Stranded colorwork pattern in the round

Work all rnds in st st, following the appropriate chart. Repeat the pattern repeat throughout the round.

Colorwork Chart 1: The pattern repeat is initially 12 sts wide. Work Rnds 1–11 once. In Rnds 6 and 10, increase as shown.

Colorwork Chart 2: The pattern repeat is initially 11 sts wide. Work Rnds 1–59 once. In Rnds 6, 10, 14, and 15, increase as shown.

Colorwork Chart 3: The pattern repeat is 16 sts wide. Repeat Rnds 1–26.

TIP

First, read through all the instructions and mark all numbers pertaining to the size you want to knit. This way, you are prepared in advance and don't have to search for the correct numbers while knitting.

⌃⌃

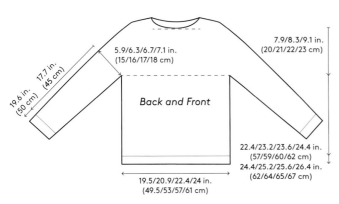

Back and Front

17.7 in. (45 cm)

19.6 in. (50 cm)

5.9/6.3/6.7/7.1 in. (15/16/17/18 cm)

7.9/8.3/9.1 in. (20/21/22/23 cm)

22.4/23.2/23.6/24.4 in. (57/59/60/62 cm)
24.4/25.2/25.6/26.4 in. (62/64/65/67 cm)

19.5/20.9/22.4/24 in. (49.5/53/57/61 cm)

INSTRUCTIONS

Using shorter circular needle size US 4 (3.5 mm) and MC, CO 76/76/80/80 sts. Join in the round and place a marker for the BoR (middle of the Back). Work 10 rnds in ribbing pattern.

Change to short circular needle size US 6 (4.0 mm), and still in MC, work 1 rnd in st st.

Now, begin increases as follows:

Sizes S and M:

Inc Rnd 1: *K2, M1L, rep from * to end of rnd (= 114 sts).

Inc Rnds 2 and 3: Work in st st, increasing a total of 3 sts during these 2 rnds, evenly distributed (= 117 sts).

Sizes L and XL:

Inc Rnd 1: *K2, M1L, rep from * to end of rnd (= 120 sts).
Work 1 rnd in st st.

Inc Rnd 2: *K5, M1L, rep from * to end of rnd (= 144 sts).

All Sizes:

Work short rows as follows:

Row 1 (RS): Beginning at the BoR (center back), k32/34/36/38, turn work.

Row 2 (WS): DSt, purl to center back, purl an additional 32/34/36/38 sts, turn work.

Row 3 (RS): DSt, knit to 3 sts after the last DSt, knitting both legs of the DSt as one when you encounter it, turn work.

Row 4 (WS): DSt, purl to 3 sts after the last DSt, purling both legs of the DSt as one when you encounter it, turn work.

Rep the last two rows (Rows 3 and 4) once, for a total of 3 DSts worked on each side. Knit for 2 rnds.

Now, work increases again as follows:

Size S:

Inc Rnd 4: *K3, M1L, rep from * to end of rnd (= 156 sts).

Inc Rnd 5: *K13, M1L, rep from * to end of rnd (= 168 sts).

Size M:

Inc Rnd 4: K1, [k2, M1L] 58 times (= 175 sts).

Inc Rnd 5: *K35, M1L, rep from * to end of rnd (= 180 sts).

Size L:

Inc Rnd 3: *K3, M1L, rep from * to end of rnd (= 192 sts).

Size XL:

Inc Rnd 3: *K3, M1L, rep from * to end of rnd (= 192 sts).

Inc Rnd 4: *K16, M1L, rep from * to end of rnd (= 204 sts).

Change to short circular needle size US 8 (5.0 mm).

Work the stranded colorwork pattern from Colorwork Chart 1. Work the pattern repeat [initially 12 sts wide] 14/15/16/17 times per round (= 168/180/192/204 sts). Work Rnds 1–11 once, increasing in Rnds 6 and 10 as shown. After Rnd 10, 14/15/16/17 pattern repeats [each 14 sts wide] will be worked per round (= 196/210/224/238 sts).

Now, continue in MC, working the next set of increases as follows:

Size S:

Inc Rnd 6: K1, [k15, M1L] 13 times (= 209 sts).

Size M:

Inc Rnd 6: *K21, M1L, rep from * to end of rnd (= 220 sts).

Size L:

Inc Rnd 4: *K32, M1L, rep from * to end of rnd (= 231 sts).

Size XL:

Inc Rnd 5: K1, [k59, M1L] 4 times, k1 (= 242 sts).

All Sizes:

Work the stranded colorwork pattern from Colorwork Chart 2. Work the pattern repeat [initially 11 sts wide] 19/20/21/22 times per round (= 209/220/231/242 sts). Work Rnds 1–59 once, increasing in Rnds 6, 10, 14, and 15 as shown. After Rnd 15, there will be 19/20/21/22 pattern repeats [each 16 sts wide] per round (= 304/320/336/352 sts). If needed, change to long circular needle size US 8 (5.0 mm) to accommodate the larger stitch count.

AT THE SAME TIME, at overall height of 7.9/8.3/8.7/9 in. (20/21/22/23 cm) from CO center front (Colorwork Chart 2 should have been worked to Rnd 24/26/28/30), in Rnd 25/27/29/31 of the colorwork chart, divide sts for Body and Sleeves as follows:

Starting at center back, k48/51/54/57 Back sts, place 56/58/60/62 Sleeve sts on holder, CO 4/5/6/7 new sts, place m (= new BoR), CO 4/5/6/7 new sts, k96/102/108/114 Front sts, place 56/58/60/62 Sleeve sts on holder, CO 8/10/12/14 new sts, k48/51/54/57 Back sts to center back.

You now have 56/58/60/62 sts + 8/10/12/14 sts for each Sleeve = 64/68/72/76 sts. Front and Back each have 96/102/108/114 sts + 16/20/24/28 sts = 208/224/240/256 total Body sts on the needles.

Finish the stranded colorwork pattern, working from Colorwork Chart 2.

Now, continue in stranded colorwork pattern from Colorwork Chart 3. Work the pattern repeat [16 sts wide] 13/14/15/16 times per round = 208/224/240/256 sts. Repeat Rnds 1–26 throughout. It is recommended to work rounds with stranded colorwork pattern using needle size US 7 (4.5 mm) and rounds without colorwork pattern on US 6 (4.0 mm) needles. During the rounds without colorwork pattern, do not carry CC throughout the round, instead using it only in actual colorwork rounds, carrying it up, and locking colors at the BoR.

When the Body measures 14.6/15/15/15.4 in. (37/38/38/39 cm) from Sleeve, work at least 3 more rnds in MC (without colorwork pattern), then break the working yarn in CC. Continue in MC with circular needle size US 4 (3.5 mm), working in ribbing pattern for 2 in. (5 cm). Bind off all sts using elastic BO method.

SLEEVES (MAKE 2)

PLEASE NOTE: To avoid unsightly holes, pick up 1 additional (unlisted) st to each side of the armhole, using the same color as the adjoining Sleeve st. In the following round, knit each of the 2 extra sts together with the corresponding Sleeve st to return to the original stitch count.

Take up the formerly held 56/58/60/62 Sleeve sts with a size US 7 (4.5 mm) DPN set, and finish the stranded colorwork pattern, working from Colorwork Chart 2. For this, beginning at the center of the additionally CO sts of the Body, work 8/10/12/14 sts (+ 1 additionally picked up st for hole prevention, as noted) for the Sleeve into the corresponding sts at the Body; knit the Sleeve sts; into the corresponding additionally CO sts at the Body, work 8/10/12/14 sts (+ 1 additionally picked up st for

hole prevention) for the Sleeve, place m (= BoR); in the following round, knit the 2 extra sts together with the adjoining sts as described above (= 64/68/72/76 sts).

Work the stranded colorwork pattern from Colorwork Chart 3. For Size S, work the pattern repeat [16 sts wide] 4 times per round; for size M, add 1 Black st per repeat [17 sts wide]; for size L add 2 Black sts per repeat [18 sts wide]; and for size XL add 3 Black sts per repeat [19 sts wide], working the repeat 4 times around. Decreases take place AT THE SAME TIME; as stitch count becomes smaller, there will be an incomplete pattern repeat at the end of the rnd. Repeat Rnds 1–26 throughout.

It is recommended to work rounds with stranded colorwork pattern using needle size US 7 (4.5 mm) and rounds without colorwork pattern on US 6 (4.0 mm) needles. During the rounds without colorwork pattern, do not carry CC throughout the round, instead using it only in actual colorwork rounds, carrying it up, and locking colors at the BoR.

When piece has reached 3.2 in. (8 cm) from begin of Sleeve, work first round of sleeve tapering decreases as follows: k2, k2tog, knit to 4 sts before m, skp, k2 (= 62/66/70/74 sts).

Repeat decreases in every 12th rnd 7 times more (= 48/52/56/60 sts).

Continue in st st in the round, working until sleeve either measures approx. 17.7 in. (45 cm) or is 2 in. (5 cm) shorter than desired length. You should have worked at least 3 rnds in MC (without colorwork pattern). Break the working yarn in CC, and continue in MC with DPN set size US 4 (3.5 mm), working in ribbing pattern for 2 in. (5 cm). Bind off all sts using elastic BO method.

FINISHING

Neatly weave in all ends. Turn the garment inside out, gently pin it into shape on an even horizontal surface, cover it with a moistened cloth, and let it dry.

COLORWORK CHART 1

14 13 12 11 10 9 8 7 6 5 4 3 2 1

11 10 9 8 7 6 5 4 3 2 1

pattern repeat at
begin = 12 sts

COLORWORK CHART 2

16 15 14 13 12 11 10 9 8 7 6 5 4 3 2 1

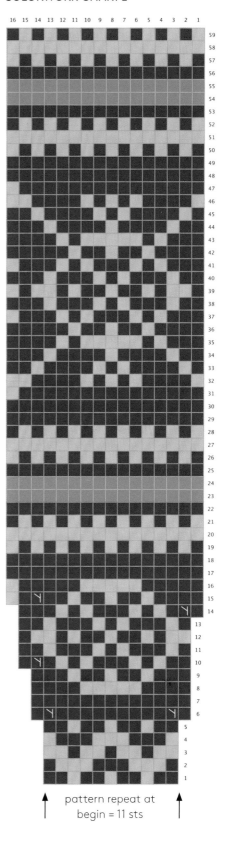

pattern repeat at
begin = 11 sts

COLORWORK CHART 3

16 15 14 13 12 11 10 9 8 7 6 5 4 3 2 1

26 25 24 23 22 21 20 19 18 17 16 15 14 13 12 11 10 9 8 7 6 5 4 3 2 1

pattern repeat = 16 sts (S),
17 sts (M), 18 sts (L), 19 sts (XL)

LEGEND

■ = MC: Black

▨ = CC1: Gray

▨ = CC2: Petrol

Υ = M1L

EYGLÓ
Short-sleeve sweater with lace-and-nupp pattern

Loose Fit
Shown in size S

SIZES

S, M, L, XL

Positive ease of at least 7.1 in. (18 cm) has already been incorporated.

PLEASE NOTE: Numbers for individual sizes are listed in order from smallest to largest size, divided by slashes. If only one number is given, it applies to all sizes.

Chest circumference: 40.6/43.7/47.6/52 in. (103/111/121/132 cm)

Sleeve width: 6.1/6.6/6.9/7.1 in. (15.5/16.75/17.5/18 cm)

MATERIALS

- ◆ Rohrspatz & Wollmeise Blend; #2 fine weight; 70% superwash merino wool, 20% cashmere, 10% poly-amide; 546 yd. (499 m) per 5.3 oz. (150 g); 2/3/3/3 skeins Himmelblau (Sky Blue)

PLEASE NOTE: Check the ball bands, and only use skeins of the same dye lot together. Actual total yardage may vary, depending on individual knitting style.

- ◆ circular needle size US 1.5 (2.5 mm), 16 in. (40 cm) long
- ◆ 2 circular needles size US 2.5 (3.0 mm), 24 in. (60 cm) and 32 in. (80 cm) long
- ◆ DPN set size US 2.5 (3.0 mm)
- ◆ tapestry needle for weaving in ends
- ◆ stitch markers
- ◆ stitch holders or waste yarn

GAUGE

Stockinette stitch on US 2.5 (3.0 mm) needles:
26 sts and 34 rows/rounds = 4 x 4 in. (10 x 10 cm)

STITCH PATTERNS

Ribbing pattern in the round

Alternate "k2, p2" to end of round.

Stockinette stitch in the round

Knit all stitches in all rounds.

Nupp pattern

Work all rnds from Knitting Chart 1. Repeat the pattern repeat [9 sts wide] throughout the round. Work Rnds 1–15 once.

Lace pattern

Work all rnds from Knitting Chart 2. Repeat the pattern repeat [initially 12 sts wide] throughout the round. Work Rnds 1–34 once, while increasing as shown (according to instructions).

Nupp-and-lace pattern

Work all rnds from Knitting Chart 3. Repeat the pattern repeat [18 sts wide] throughout the round. Work Rnds 1–15 once.

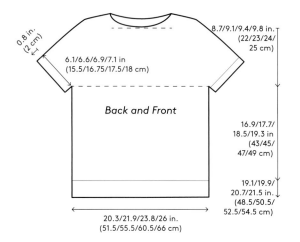

8.7/9.1/9.4/9.8 in.
(22/23/24/25 cm)

6.1/6.6/6.9/7.1 in
(15.5/16.75/17.5/18 cm)

0.8 in.
(2 cm)

Back and Front

16.9/17.7/18.5/19.3 in
(43/45/47/49 cm)

19.1/19.9/20.7/21.5 in.
(48.5/50.5/52.5/54.5 cm)

20.3/21.9/23.8/26 in.
(51.5/55.5/60.5/66 cm)

INSTRUCTIONS

Using circular needle size US 1.5 (2.5 mm), CO 136/144/144/152 sts. Join in the round and place a marker for the BoR (middle of the Back). Work 4 rnds in ribbing pattern.

Change to short circular needle size US 2.5 (3.0 mm), and begin increases as follows:

Size S:

Inc Rnd 1: K2, M1L, [k4, M1L] 33 times, k2, M1L (= 171 sts).

Size M:

Inc Rnd 1: *K4, M1L, rep from * to end of rnd (= 180 sts).

Size L:

Inc Rnd 1: K5, [k3, M1L] 45 times, k4 (= 189 sts).

Size XL:

Inc Rnd 1: *K4, M1L, rep from * to end of rnd (= 190 sts).

Inc Rnd 2: K3, [k23, M1L] 8 times, k3 (= 198 sts).

All Sizes:

Work 3 rnds in st st.

Work short rows as follows:

Row 1 (RS): Beginning at the BoR (center back), k54/54/58/58, turn work.

Row 2 (WS): DSt, purl to center back, purl an additional 54/54/58/58 sts again, turn work.

Row 3 (RS): DSt, knit to 5 sts after the last DSt, knitting both legs of the DSt together as one, turn work.

Row 4 (WS): DSt, purl to 5 sts after the last DSt, purling both legs of the DSt together as one, turn work.

Repeat the last two rows (Rows 3 and 4) twice; there will be a total of 4 DSts per side.

Then, knit 1 rnd, knitting both legs of the DSt as one when you encounter it.

Work the nupp pattern from Knitting Chart 1. Work the pattern repeat [9 sts wide] 19/20/21/22 times per round, work Rnds 1–15 once.

After having completed the nupp pattern, for all sizes, work the next inc rnd as follows:

Inc Rnd 2/2/2/3: *K3, yo, rep from * to end of rnd (= 228/240/252/264 sts).

Now, work the lace pattern from Knitting Chart 2. Work the pattern repeat [initially 12 sts wide] 19/20/21/22 times per round. Work Rnds 1–34 once, while increasing as shown.

NOTE ABOUT THE CHART (FOR ALL SIZES):

In Rnd 9 of the chart (= Inc Rnd 3/3/3/4), every pattern repeat adds 2 sts. These increases are created by yarn overs. In this round, there are no accompanying decreases (= 19/20/21/22 pattern repeats [each 14 sts wide] = 266/280/294/308 sts).

In Rnd 18 of the chart (= Inc Rnd 4/4/4/5), every pattern repeat adds 1 st. These increases are created by working M1L (= 19/20/21/22 pattern repeats [each 15 sts wide] = 285/300/315/330 sts).

After having completed the lace pattern, work the next inc rnd as follows:

Inc Rnd 5/5/5/6: *K3, yo, rep from * to end of rnd (= 380/400/420/440 sts).

Now, to adjust the stitch count for the following nupp-and-lace pattern, work the next rnd as follows:

Size S:

Next Rnd: K2tog, k85, k2tog, k to end of rnd (= 378 sts).

Size M:

Next Rnd: K4, [k28, M1L] 14 times, k4 (= 414 sts).

Size L:

Next Rnd: *K14, M1L, rep from * to end of rnd (= 450 sts).

Size XL:

Next Rnd: * M1L, [k10, M1L] 22 times, rep from * once (= 486 sts).

All Sizes:

Work 2 rnds in st st.

Now, work the nupp-and-lace pattern from Knitting Chart 3. Work the pattern repeat [18 sts wide] 21/23/25/27 times per round, work Rnds 1–15 once.

After having completed the nupp-and-lace pattern, if required, continue in st st until an overall height of 8.7/9/9.5/9.8 in. (22/23/24/25 cm) from CO center front has been reached. Then, divide sts for Body and Sleeves as follows:

Starting at center back, k61/66/73/80 Back sts, place 69/75/79/83 Sleeve sts on holder, CO 6 new sts, place m (= new BoR), CO 6 new sts, k120/132/146/160 Front sts, place 69/75/79/83 Sleeve sts on holder, CO 12 new sts, k59/66/73/80 Back sts to center back.

You now have 69/75/79/83 sts + 12 sts = 81/87/91/95 sts for each Sleeve. Front and Back each have 120/132/146/160 sts + 24 sts = 264/288/316/344 total Body sts on the needles.

Continue the Body in st st in the round, working until Body measures 8.3/8.7/9/9.5 in. (21/22/23/24 cm) from Sleeve. Change to size US 1.5 (2.5 mm) needles and work 2.2 in. (5.5 cm) in ribbing pattern. Bind off all sts using elastic BO method.

SLEEVES (MAKE 2)

PLEASE NOTE: To avoid unsightly holes, 1 additional (unlisted) stitch should be picked up at each side of the armhole. In the following round, knit each of the 2 extra sts together with the corresponding Sleeve stitch to return to the original stitch count.

Take up the formerly held 69/75/79/83 Sleeve sts with a DPN set in size US 1.5 (2.5 mm). For the armhole, beginning at the center of the additionally CO sts of the Body, work 6 sts (+ 1 additionally picked up st for hole prevention, as noted) for the Sleeve into the corresponding sts at the Body; knit the Sleeve sts; into the corresponding additionally CO sts at the Body, work 6 sts (+ 1 additionally picked up st for hole prevention) for the Sleeves, place m (= BoR); in the following round, knit the 2 extra sts together with the adjoining sts as described above (= 81/87/91/95 sts).

Knit 1 rnd, adjusting the stitch count before the ribbing pattern as follows for your size:

Size S:

Decrease 1 st (= 80 sts).

Sizes M, L, XL:

Increase 1 st (= 88/92/96 sts).

Work 4 rnds in ribbing pattern. Then bind off all sts using elastic BO method.

FINISHING

Neatly weave in all ends. Turn the garment inside out, gently pin it into shape on an even horizontal surface, cover it with a moistened cloth, and let it dry.

KNITTING CHART 1 – NUPP PATTERN

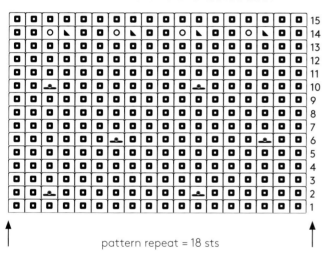

pattern repeat = 9 sts

KNITTING CHART 2 – LACE PATTERN

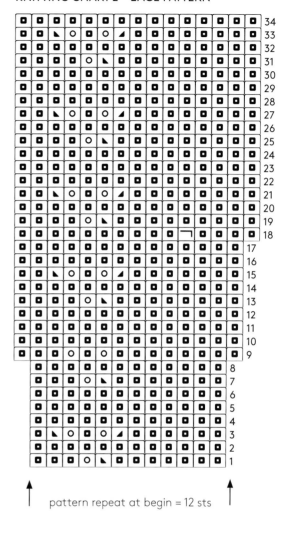

pattern repeat at begin = 12 sts

KNITTING CHART 3 – NUPP-AND-LACE PATTERN

pattern repeat = 18 sts

LEGEND

▣	= knit 1
○	= 1 yarn over
⌐	= M1L
◢	= k2tog
◣	= skp (= slip 1, k1, then pass the slipped st over the knitted one)
♠	= Nupp: Make 4 sts from 1 as follows: Work [k1, p1, k1, p1] into the same stitch. Turn work. Purl the same 4 sts. Turn work. Place the working yarn in back of work, and slip the first 3 sts together as if to purl. Now, knit the 4th st and then, one after another, pass the 3 formerly slipped sts over the knitted one (= 1 st).

HAFRÚN
Sweater in a stranded colorwork pattern

◆◆◆

Slim Fit
Shown in size S

SIZES

S, M, L, XL

Positive ease of approx. 2.4 in. (6 cm) has already been incorporated.

PLEASE NOTE: Numbers for individual sizes are listed in order from smallest to largest size, divided by slashes. If only one number is given, it applies to all sizes.

Chest circumference: 35.8/39/41.3/44.1 in. (91/99/105/112 cm)

Sleeve width: 5.5/5.9/6.3/7.1 in. (14/15/16/17.5 cm)

MATERIALS

◆ Isager Alpaca 2; #1 super fine weight; 50% alpaca, 50% wool; 273 yd. (250 m) per 1.75 oz. (50 g); 5/5/6/6 skeins #36 Dunkelrot (Dark Red) and 1 skein each #Eco-0 Weiß (White), #Eco-7s Braun (Brown), #24 Orange, and #21 Rostrot (Rust Brown)

PLEASE NOTE: Check the ball bands, and only use skeins of the same dye lot together. Actual total yardage may vary, depending on individual knitting style.

◆ circular needle size US 1.5 (2.5 mm), 16 in. (40 cm) long

◆ 2 circular needles size US 2.5 (3.0 mm), 16 in. (40 cm) and 32 in. (80 cm) long

◆ 2 circular needles size US 6 (4.0 mm), 24 in. (60 cm) and 32 in. (80 cm) long

◆ DPN sets sizes US 1.5 (2.5 mm), US 2.5 (3.0 mm), and US 6 (4.0 mm)

◆ tapestry needle for weaving in ends

◆ stitch markers

◆ stitch holders or waste yarn

GAUGE

Stockinette stitch in one color on US 2.5 (3.0 mm) needles: 32 sts and 40 rows/rounds = 4 x 4 in. (10 x 10 cm)

PLEASE NOTE: Since everybody knits differently, the stranded colorwork pattern should be swatched to determine whether a smaller or larger needle size might be required to match the listed gauge. Needle size US 6 (4.0 mm) is recommended.

COLOR DESIGNATIONS

MC: Dark Red

CC1: White

CC2: Brown

CC3: Orange

CC4: Rust Brown

STITCH PATTERNS

Ribbing pattern in the round

Alternate "k2, p2" to end of round.

Stockinette stitch in the round

Knit all stitches in all rounds.

TIP

First, read through all the instructions and mark all numbers pertaining to the size you want to knit. This way, you are prepared in advance and don't have to search for the correct numbers while knitting.

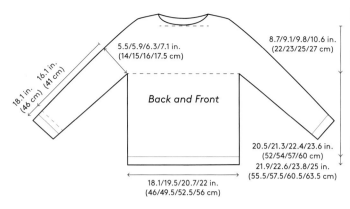

5.5/5.9/6.3/7.1 in.
(14/15/16/17.5 cm)

8.7/9.1/9.8/10.6 in.
(22/23/25/27 cm)

18.1 in. 16.1 in.
(46 cm) (41 cm)

Back and Front

20.5/21.3/22.4/23.6 in.
(52/54/57/60 cm)
21.9/22.6/23.8/25 in.
(55.5/57.5/60.5/63.5 cm)

18.1/19.5/20.7/22 in.
(46/49.5/52.5/56 cm)

INSTRUCTIONS

Using circular needle size US 1.5 (2.5 mm) and MC, CO 120/124/124/128 sts. Join in the round and place a marker for the BoR (middle of the Back). Work 14 rnds in ribbing pattern.

Change to short circular needle size US 2.5 (3.0 mm), and knit 1 rnd.

Work short rows as follows:

Row 1 (RS): K24/26/26/30, turn work.

Row 2 (WS): DSt, purl to center back, purl an additional 24/26/26/30 sts, turn work.

Row 3 (RS): DSt, knit to center back, [k3, M1L] 5 times, knit to DSt, knitting both legs of the DSt as one when you encounter it, k2, turn work (= 125/129/129/133 sts).

Row 4 (WS): DSt, purl to center back, [p3, M1R] 5 times, purl to DSt, purling both legs of the DSt as one when you encounter it, p2, turn work (= 130/134/134/138 sts).

Row 5 (RS): DSt, knit to center back, knit to DSt, knitting both legs of the DSt as one when you encounter it, k1, turn work.

Row 6 (WS): DSt, purl to center back, purl to DSt, purling both legs of the DSt as one when you encounter it, p1, turn work.

Repeat the last two rows (Rows 5 and 6) twice.

Next Row (RS): DSt, knit to center back.

Knit 1 rnd; knit both legs of the DSt as one when you encounter it.

Now, resume working in the round and begin increases as follows:

Size S:

Inc Rnd 1: K2, [k9, M1L] 14 times, k2 (=144 sts).

Work 3 rnds in st st.

Size M:

Inc Rnd 1: K1, [k6, M1L] 22 times, k1 (= 156 sts).

Size L:

Inc Rnd 1: K1, [k4, M1L] 31 times (= 156 sts).

Inc Rnd 2: [K13, M1L] 12 times (= 168 sts).

Work 3 rnds in st st.

Size XL:

Inc Rnd 1: K5, [k4, M1L] 32 times, k5 (= 170 sts).

Inc Rnd 2: *K17, M1L, rep from * to end of rnd (= 180 sts).

Work 3 rnds in st st.

All Sizes:

Change to short circular needle size US 6 (4.0 mm), and continue as follows:

Work stranded colorwork pattern from colorwork chart. Work the pattern repeat [initially 6 sts wide] 24/26/28/30 times per round (= 144/156/168/180 sts). Work Rnds 1–52 once, increasing as shown in Rnds 9, 12, 20, 24, 30, 38, 45, and 47. Now, in each round, 24/26/28/30 pattern repeats [each 16 sts wide] will be worked (= 384/416/448/480 sts). If needed, change to long circular needle size US 6 (4.0 mm) to accommodate the larger stitch count.

After having completed the colorwork pattern, change to circular needle size US 2.5 (3.0 mm), break the working yarn in CC, and continue in MC only.

At overall height of 8.7/9/9.8/10.7 in. (22/23/25/27 cm) from CO center front, divide sts for Body and Sleeves as follows:

Starting at center back, k62/67/72/77 Back sts, place 68/74/80/86 Sleeve sts on holder, CO 11/12/12/13 new sts, place m (= new BoR), CO 11/12/12/13 new sts, k124/134/144/154 Front sts, place 68/74/80/86 Sleeve sts on holder, CO 22/24/24/26 new sts, k62/67/72/77 Back sts to center back.

You now have 68/74/80/86 sts + 22/24/24/26 sts = 90/98/104/112 sts for each Sleeve. Front and Back each have 124/134/144/154 sts + 44/48/48/52 sts = 292/316/336/360 total Body sts on the needles.

Continue in st st, working until Body measures 11.8/12.2/12.6/13 in. (30/31/32/33 cm) from Sleeve. Change to US 1.5 (2.5 mm) needles and work 14 rnds in ribbing pattern. Bind off all sts using elastic BO method.

SLEEVES (MAKE 2)

PLEASE NOTE: To avoid unsightly holes, 1 additional (unlisted) stitch should be picked up at each side of the armhole. In the following round, knit each of the 2 extra sts together with the corresponding Sleeve st to return to the original stitch count.

Take up the formerly held 68/74/80/86 Sleeve sts with DPN set size US 2.5 (3.0 mm). For the armhole, beginning at the center of the additionally CO sts of the Body, work 11/12/12/13 sts (+1 additionally picked up st for hole prevention, as noted) for the Sleeve into the corresponding sts at the Body; knit the Sleeve sts; into the corresponding additionally CO sts at the Body, work 11/12/12/13 sts (+1 additionally picked up st for hole prevention) for the Sleeve, place m (= BoR); in the following round, knit the 2 extra sts together with the adjoining sts as described above (= 90/98/104/112 Sleeve sts).

Continue in st st in the round. When piece has reached 3.2 in. (8 cm) from begin of Sleeve, work first sleeve tapering dec rnd as follows: k2, k2tog, knit to 4 sts before m, skp, k2 (= 2 sts decreased = 88/96/102/110 sts).

Repeat decreases 10/13/15/18 times more in every 12th/9th/8th/7th rnd (= 68/70/72/74 sts).

Continue in st st in the round, working until Sleeve either measures approx. 16.1 in. (41 cm) or is 2 in. (5 cm) shorter than desired length.

For **sizes M and XL**, adjust the stitch count for the stranded colorwork pattern as follows: k2, k2tog, knit to 4 sts before m, skp, k2 (= 68/68/72/72 sts).

Now, using DPN set size US 6 (4.0 mm), work Rnds 49–52 of the colorwork chart, always repeating only the first 4 sts of the pattern repeat.

Change to size US 2.5 (3.0 mm) needles and work 2 rnds more in MC in st st. Then change to DPN set size US 1.5 (2.5 mm) and work 14 rnds in ribbing pattern. Bind off all sts using elastic BO method.

FINISHING

Neatly weave in all ends. Turn the garment inside out, gently pin it into shape on an even horizontal surface, cover it with a moistened cloth, and let it dry.

LEGEND

■ = MC: Dark Red   ▨ = CC3: Orange

□ = CC1: White   ■ = CC4: Rust Brown

▨ = CC2: Brown   ⅄ = M1L

COLORWORK CHART

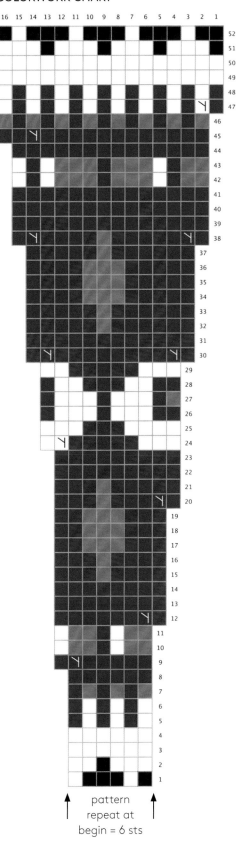

pattern repeat at begin = 6 sts

HJÖRDÍS

Sweater in a stranded colorwork pattern

◆◆◆

Loose Fit
Shown in
size M

SIZES

S, M, L, XL

Positive ease of at least 7.1 in. (18 cm) has already been incorporated.

PLEASE NOTE: Numbers for individual sizes are listed in order from smallest to largest size, divided by slashes. If only one number is given, it applies to all sizes.

Chest circumference: 42.5/45.3/48.8/52.4 in. (108/115/124/133 cm)

Sleeve width: 6.5/6.7/7/7.3 in. (16.5/17/18/18.5 cm)

MATERIALS

◆ Isager Alpaca 2; #1 super fine weight; 50% alpaca, 50% wool; 273 yd. (250 m) per 1.75 oz. (50 g); 6/7/8/9 skeins #Eco-7s Braun (Brown) and 1 skein each #59 Gold, #3 Ocker (Ochre), #21 Rot (Red), and #Eco-4s Dunkelbraun (Dark Brown)

PLEASE NOTE: Check the ball bands, and only use skeins of the same dye lot together. Actual total yardage may vary, depending on individual knitting style.

◆ circular needle size US 1.5 (2.5 mm), 16 in. (40 cm) long
◆ 2 circular needles size US 2.5 (3.0 mm), 16 in. (40 cm) and 32 in. (80 cm) long
◆ 2 circular needles size US 6 (4.0 mm), 24 in. (60 cm) and 32 in. (80 cm) long
◆ DPN sets in sizes US 1.5 (2.5 mm) and US 2.5 (3.0 mm)
◆ tapestry needle for weaving in ends
◆ stitch markers
◆ stitch holders or waste yarn

GAUGE

Stockinette stitch in one color on US 2.5 (3.0 mm) needles: 32 sts and 40 rows/rounds = 4 x 4 in. (10 x 10 cm)

PLEASE NOTE: Since everybody knits differently, the stranded colorwork pattern should be swatched to determine whether a smaller or larger needle size might be required to match the listed gauge. Needle size US 6 (4.0 mm) is recommended.

COLOR DESIGNATIONS

MC: Brown

CC1: Gold

CC2: Ochre

CC3: Red

CC4: Dark Brown

STITCH PATTERNS

Ribbing pattern in the round

Alternate "k2, p2" to end of round.

Stockinette stitch in the round

Knit all stitches in all rounds.

Stranded colorwork pattern in the round

Work all rnds in st st, following the appropriate chart. Repeat the pattern repeat throughout the round.

Colorwork Chart 1: The pattern repeat is 6 sts wide. Work Rnds 1–7 once.

Colorwork Chart 2: The pattern repeat is initially 14 sts wide. Work Rnds 1–45 once. In Rnds 5, 11, 19, 25, 33, and 34, increase as shown.

Colorwork Chart 3: The pattern repeat is 5 sts wide. Work Rnds 1–7 once.

PLEASE NOTE: Lock in floats after every 3rd stitch. Keep CC at the base of the finger, i.e., in front.

TIP

First, read through all the instructions and mark all numbers pertaining to the size you want to knit. This way, you are prepared in advance and don't have to search for the correct numbers while knitting.

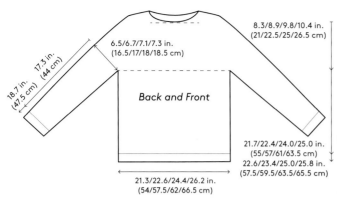

6.5/6.7/7.1/7.3 in.
(16.5/17/18/18.5 cm)

8.3/8.9/9.8/10.4 in.
(21/22.5/25/26.5 cm)

17.3 in.
(44 cm)

18.7 in.
(47.5 cm)

Back and Front

21.7/22.4/24.0/25.0 in.
(55/57/61/63.5 cm)

22.6/23.4/25.0/25.8 in.
(57.5/59.5/63.5/65.5 cm)

21.3/22.6/24.4/26.2 in.
(54/57.5/62/66.5 cm)

INSTRUCTIONS

Using circular needle size US 1.5 (2.5 mm) and MC, CO 124/132/140/148 sts. Join in the round and place a marker for the BoR (middle of the Back). Work 14 rnds in ribbing pattern.

Change to shorter circular needle size US 2.5 (3.0 mm), and knit 1 rnd.

Now, work Inc Rnd 1 as follows:

Size S:

Inc Rnd 1: *K2, M1L, rep from * to end of rnd (= 186 sts).

Size M:

Inc Rnd 1: *K2, M1L, rep from * to end of rnd (= 198 sts).

Size L:

Inc Rnd 1: *K2, M1L, rep from * to end of rnd (= 210 sts).

Size XL:

Inc Rnd 1: *K2, M1L, rep from * to end of rnd (= 222 sts).

All Sizes:

Work 1 rnd in st st.

Work short rows as follows:

Row 1 (RS): Beginning at the BoR (center back), k54/58/62/66, turn work.

Row 2 (WS): DSt, purl to center back, purl an additional 54/58/62/66 sts, turn work.

Row 3 (RS): DSt, knit to 3 sts after the last DSt, knit both legs of the DSt as one, turn work.

Row 4 (WS): DSt, purl to 3 sts after the last DSt, purl both legs of the DSt as one, turn work.

Repeat the last two rows (Rows 3 and 4) twice; there will be a total of 4 DSts per side.

Now, knit 2 rnds.

Change to short circular needle size US 6 (4.0 mm).

Work the stranded colorwork pattern from Colorwork Chart 1. Work the pattern repeat [6 sts wide] 31/33/35/37 times per round (= 186/198/210/222 sts). Work Rnds 1–7 once.

Then, work the next set of increases in MC:

Size S:

Inc Rnd 2: M1L, *k2, M1L, rep from * to end of rnd (= 280 sts).

Size M:

Inc Rnd 2: M1L, *k2, M1L, rep from * to end of rnd (= 298 sts).

Inc Rnd 3: K4, [k29, M1L] 10 times, k4 (= 308 sts).

Size L:

Inc Rnd 2: M1L, *k2, M1L, rep from * to end of rnd (= 316 sts).

Inc Rnd 3: K8, [k15, M1L] 20 times, k8 (= 336 sts).

Size XL:

Inc Rnd 2: M1L, *k2, M1L, rep from * to end of rnd (= 334 sts).

Inc Rnd 3: K2, [k11, M1L] 30 times, k2 (= 364 sts).

All sizes:

Work the stranded colorwork pattern from Colorwork Chart 2. Work the pattern repeat [initially 14 sts wide] 20/22/24/26 times per round (= 280/308/336/364 sts). Work Rnds 1–45 once, increasing in Rnds 5, 11, 19, 25, and 33 as shown. After Rnd 33, there will be 20/22/24/26 pattern repeats [each 23 sts wide] (= 460/506/552/598 sts).

Then, work the next set of increases in MC:

Size S:

Inc Rnd 3: *K10, M1L, rep from * to end of rnd (= 506 sts).

Inc Rnd 4: K3, [k125, M1L] 4 times, k3 (= 510 sts).

Size M:

Inc Rnd 4: K5, [k15, M1L] 33 times, k6 (= 540 sts).

Size L:

Inc Rnd 4: K6, [k30, M1L] 18 times, k6 (= 570 sts).

Size XL:

Inc Rnd 4: *K299, M1L, rep from * once (= 600 sts).

Work the stranded colorwork pattern from Colorwork Chart 3. Work the pattern repeat [5 sts wide] 102/108/114/120 times per round (= 510/540/570/600 sts). Work Rnds 1–7 once.

Then, change to circular needle size US 2.5 (3.0 mm), break the working yarn in CC, and continue in MC only.

At overall height of 8.3/8.9/9.8/10.4 in. (21/22.5/25/26.5 cm) from CO center front, divide sts for Body and Sleeves as follows:

Starting at center back, k80/86/92/99 Back sts, place 94/98/100/102 Sleeve sts on holder, CO 6/6/7/8 new sts, place m (= new BoR), CO 6/6/7/8 new sts, k162/172/185/198 Front sts, place 94/98/100/102 Sleeve sts on holder, CO 12/12/14/16 new sts, k80/86/93/99 Back sts to center back.

You now have 94/98/100/102 sts + 12/12/14/16 sts = 106/110/114/118 sts for each Sleeve. Front and Back each have 162/172/185/198 sts + 24/24/28/32 sts = 348/368/398/428 total Body sts on the needles.

Continue in st st, working until Body measures 13.4/13.8/14.2/14.6 in. (34/35/36/37 cm) from Sleeve. Change to US 1.5 (2.5 mm) needles and work 14 rnds in ribbing pattern. Bind off all sts using elastic BO method.

SLEEVES (MAKE 2)

PLEASE NOTE: To avoid unsightly holes, 1 additional (unlisted) stitch should be picked up at each side of the armhole. In the following round, knit each of the 2 extra sts together with the corresponding Sleeve st to return to the original stitch count.

In MC, take up the formerly held 94/98/100/102 Sleeve sts with DPN set in size US 2.5 (3.0 mm). For the armhole, beginning at the center of the additionally CO sts of the Body, work 6/6/7/8 sts (+1 additionally picked up st for hole prevention, as noted) for the Sleeve into the corresponding sts at the Body; knit the Sleeve sts; into the corresponding additionally CO sts at the Body, work 6/6/7/8 sts (+1 additionally picked up st for hole prevention) for the Sleeve, place m (= BoR); in the following round, knit the 2 extra sts together with the adjoining sts as described above (= 106/110/114/118 sts).

Continue in st st in the round. When piece has reached 3.2 in. (8 cm) from begin of Sleeve, work first sleeve tapering dec rnd as follows: k2, k2tog, knit to 4 sts before m, skp, k2 (= 2 sts decreased = 104/108/112/116 sts).

Repeat sleeve tapering decreases in every 7th/6th/7th/6th rnd 18/20/18/20 times (= 68/68/76/76 sts).

Continue in st st in the round, working until Sleeve either measures approx. 17.3 in. (44 cm) or is 1.6 in. (4 cm) shorter than desired length. Change to DPN set in size US 1.5 (2.5 mm), and work 14 rnds in ribbing pattern. Bind off all sts using elastic BO method.

FINISHING

Neatly weave in all ends. Turn the garment inside out, gently pin it into shape on an even horizontal surface, cover it with a moistened cloth, and let it dry.

COLORWORK CHART 2

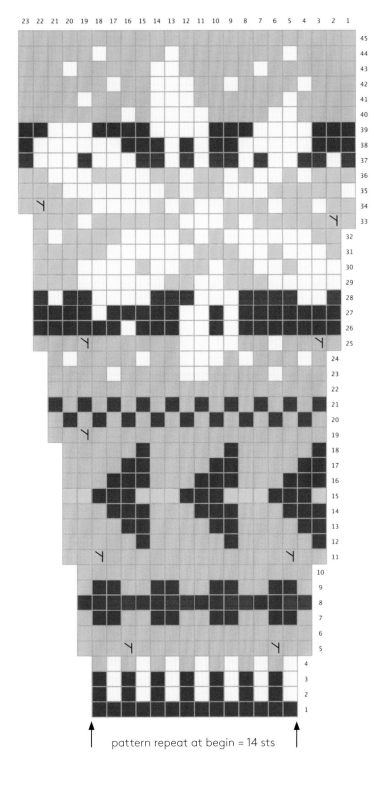

pattern repeat at begin = 14 sts

COLORWORK CHART 1

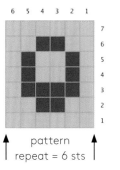

pattern
repeat = 6 sts

COLORWORK CHART 3

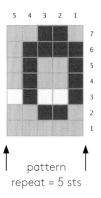

pattern
repeat = 5 sts

LEGEND

- = MC: Brown
- = CC1: Gold
- = CC2: Ochre
- = CC3: Red
- = CC4: Dark Brown
- Y = M1L

RAGNHEIDUR
Sweater with cable pattern

Regular Fit
Shown in size S

SIZES

S, M, L, XL

Positive ease of approx. 5.5 in. (14 cm) has already been incorporated.

PLEASE NOTE: Numbers for individual sizes are listed in order from smallest to largest size, divided by slashes. If only one number is given, it applies to all sizes.

Chest circumference: 41/43.3/45.7/47.7 in. (104/110/116/121 cm)

Sleeve width: 6.3/6.5/6.7/6.9 in. (16/16.5/17/17.5 cm)

MATERIALS

- Schachenmayr Cosy Wool; #4 medium weight; 64% rayon/viscose, 25% acrylic, 11% wool; 109 yd. (100 m) per 1.75 oz. (50 g); 9/10/11/12 skeins #52 Cloud and 1 skein #22 Gold

PLEASE NOTE: Check the ball bands, and only use skeins of the same dye lot together. Actual total yardage may vary, depending on individual knitting style.

- circular needle size US 7 (4.5 mm), 16 in. (40 cm) long
- 2 circular needles size US 8 (5.0 mm), 24 in. (60 cm) and 32 in. (80 cm) long
- DPN sets sizes US 7 (4.5 mm) and US 8 (5.0 mm)
- cable needle or auxiliary needle
- tapestry needle for weaving in ends
- stitch markers
- stitch holders or waste yarn

GAUGE

Garter stitch using US 8 (5.0 mm) needles: 16 sts and 32 rows/rounds = 4 x 4 in. (10 x 10 cm)

Garter stitch with cable pattern using US 8 (5.0 mm) needles: 19 sts and 30 rows/rounds = 4 x 4 in. (10 x 10 cm)

COLOR DESIGNATIONS

MC: Cloud

CC: Gold

STITCH PATTERNS

Ribbing pattern in the round

Alternate "k2, p2" in the round.

Garter stitch in the round

Rnd 1: Knit all sts (= knit rnd).

Rnd 2: Purl all sts (= purl rnd).

Repeat Rounds 1 and 2 throughout.

Cable pattern

In all rounds, work from Cable Chart. Repeat the pattern repeat [initially 10 sts wide] throughout the round. Repeat Rnds 1–16 as stated in the instructions.

PLEASE NOTE: Increases are worked at the same time—these increases are not shown in the chart, but listed in the written instructions.

TIP

First, read through all the instructions and mark all numbers pertaining to the size you want to knit. This way, you are prepared in advance and don't have to search for the correct numbers while knitting.

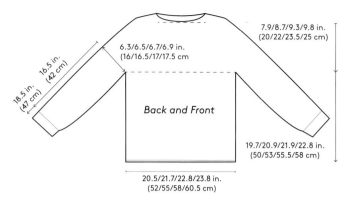

7.9/8.7/9.3/9.8 in.
(20/22/23.5/25 cm)

6.3/6.5/6.7/6.9 in.
(16/16.5/17/17.5 cm

16.5 in.
(42 cm)

18.5 in.
(47 cm)

Back and Front

19.7/20.9/21.9/22.8 in.
(50/53/55.5/58 cm)

20.5/21.7/22.8/23.8 in.
(52/55/58/60.5 cm)

INSTRUCTIONS

Using circular needle size US 7 (4.5 mm) and MC, CO 76/76/80/80 sts. Join in the round and place a marker for the BoR (middle of the Back). Work 6 rnds in ribbing pattern.

Change to short circular needle size US 8 (5.0 mm). Work in garter stitch, and begin increases as follows:

Sizes S and M:

Inc Rnd 1: K2, [k3, M1L] 24 times, k2 (= 100 sts).

Sizes L and XL:

Inc Rnd 1: *K2, M1L, rep from * to end of rnd (= 120 sts).

Inc Rnd 2: *K12, M1L, rep from * to end of rnd (= 130 sts).

All Sizes:

Work Cable pattern from chart. Work the pattern repeat [initially 10 sts wide] 10/10/13/13 times per round (= 100/100/130/130 sts).

Work Rnds 1–16 once for the first time, increasing as follows:

For all sizes:

Rnd 5 of the chart = Inc Rnd 2/2/3/3: At the end of every pattern repeat, M1L (= 110/110/143/143 sts). This increased stitch will be referred to as the "center stitch" (ctr st).

From here on, additional sts will be increased before and after this "center stitch." These increased sts will then be worked in garter stitch.

Work the first heightwise pattern repeat (= Rnds 1–16 of the chart), increasing as follows:

Size S:

Rnd 9 of the chart: In every pattern repeat, M1L before the ctr st and M1R after the ctr st from the bar between sts (= 2 sts increased in every pattern repeat = 130 sts).

Rnd 13 of the chart: In every pattern repeat, M1L before the ctr st and M1R after the ctr st from the bar between sts (= 2 sts increased in every pattern repeat = 150 sts).

Change to long circular needle size US 8 (5.0 mm).

Size M:

Rnd 9 of the chart: In every pattern repeat, M1L before the ctr st and M1R after the ctr st from the bar between sts (= 2 sts increased in every pattern repeat = 130 sts).

Rnd 13 of the chart: In every pattern repeat, after the ctr st, M1L (= 1 st increased in every pattern repeat = 140 sts).

Change to long circular needle size US 8 (5.0 mm).

Size L:

Rnd 9 of the chart: In every pattern repeat, after the ctr st, M1L (= 1 st increased in every pattern repeat = 156 sts).

Rnd 13 of the chart: In every pattern repeat, M1L before the ctr st and M1R after the ctr st from the bar between sts (= 2 sts increased in every pattern repeat = 182 sts).

Change to long circular needle size US 8 (5.0 mm).

Size XL:

Rnd 9 of the chart: In every pattern repeat, M1L before the ctr st and M1R after the ctr st from the bar between sts (= 2 sts increased in every pattern repeat = 169 sts).

Rnd 13 of the chart: In every pattern repeat, M1L before the ctr st and M1R after the ctr st from the bar between sts (= 2 sts increased in every pattern repeat = 195 sts).

Change to long circular needle size US 8 (5.0 mm).

Now, work the second heightwise pattern repeat (= Rnds 1–16 of the chart), increasing as follows:

Sizes S and M:

Rnd 1 of the chart: In every pattern repeat, M1L before the ctr st and M1R after the ctr st from the bar between sts (= 2 sts increased in every pattern repeat = 170/160 sts).

Rnd 5 of the chart: In every pattern repeat, M1L before the ctr st and M1R after the ctr st from the bar between sts (= 2 sts increased in every pattern repeat = 190/180 sts).

Rnd 9 of the chart: In every pattern repeat, M1L before the ctr st and M1R after the ctr st from the bar between sts (= 2 sts increased in every pattern repeat = 210/200 sts).

Rnd 13 of the chart: In every pattern repeat, M1L before the ctr st and M1R after the ctr st from the bar between sts (= 2 sts increased in every pattern repeat = 230/220 sts).

Sizes L and XL:

Rnd 1 of the chart: In every pattern repeat, M1L before the ctr st and M1R after the ctr st from the bar between sts (= 2 sts increased in every pattern repeat = 208/221 sts).

Rnd 5 of the chart: In every pattern repeat, M1L before the ctr st and M1R after the ctr st from the bar between sts (= 2 sts increased in every pattern repeat = 234/247 sts).

Rnd 9 of the chart: In every pattern repeat, M1L before the ctr st and M1R after the ctr st from the bar between sts (= 2 sts increased in every pattern repeat = 260/273 sts).

Rnd 13 of the chart: In every pattern repeat, after the ctr st, M1L (= 1 st increased in every pattern repeat = 273/286 sts).

The second heightwise pattern repeat ends here.

Now, begin a third heightwise pattern repeat, and work as follows:

Size S:

Rnd 1 of the chart: In every pattern repeat, after the ctr st, M1L (= 1 st increased in every pattern repeat = 240 sts).

Then, continue in Cable pattern according to chart without increases, working to an overall height of approx. 7.9 in. (20 cm) from CO center front. End with a round of all knit sts without cabling.

Size M:

Rnd 1 of the chart: In every pattern repeat, M1L before the ctr st and M1R after the ctr st from the bar between sts (= 2 sts increased in every pattern repeat = 240 sts).

Rnd 5 of the chart: In every pattern repeat, M1L before the ctr st and M1R after the ctr st from the bar between sts (= 2 sts increased in every pattern repeat = 260 sts).

Then, continue in Cable pattern according to chart without increases, working to an overall height of approx. 8.7 in. (22 cm) from CO center front. End with a round of all knit sts without cabling.

Size L:

Continue in Cable pattern according to chart to an overall height of approx. 9.3 in. (23.5 cm) from CO center front, at the same time increasing 1 st left-leaning (M1L) (= 274 sts). End with a round of all knit sts without cabling.

Size XL:

Continue in Cable pattern according to chart without increases to an overall height of approx. 10 in. (25 cm) from CO center front. End with a round of all knit sts without cabling.

All Sizes:

Divide sts for Body and Sleeves as follows:

Starting at center back, k38/41/43/46 Back sts, place 44/48/50/52 Sleeve sts on holder, CO 3 new sts, place m (= new BoR), CO 3 new sts, k76/82/87/91 Front sts, place 44/48/50/52 Sleeve sts on holder, CO 6 new sts, k38/41/44/45 Back sts to center back.

You now have 44/48/50/52 sts + 6 sts = 50/54/56/58 sts for each Sleeve. Front and Back each have 76/82/87/91 sts + 12 sts = 164/176/186/194 total Body sts on the needles.

Change to circular needle size US 8 (5.0 mm), and continue, working in garter stitch over all sts until Body measures 11.4/11.8/12.2/12.6 in. (29/30/31/32 cm) from Sleeve. Now, end with purl round, and break the working yarn in MC. Change to CC, and knit 1 rnd, then purl 1 rnd. Bind off all sts using elastic BO method.

SLEEVES (MAKE 2)

PLEASE NOTE: To avoid unsightly holes, 1 additional (unlisted) stitch should be picked up at each side of the armhole. In the following round, knit each of the 2 extra sts together with the corresponding Sleeve st to return to the original stitch count.

Take up the formerly held 44/48/50/52 Sleeve sts with a DPN set in size US 8 (5.0 mm), and work in garter stitch: For the armhole, beginning at the center of the additionally CO sts of the Body, work 3 sts (+ 1 additionally picked up st for hole prevention, as noted) for the Sleeve into the corresponding sts at the Body; knit the Sleeve sts; into the corresponding additionally CO sts at the Body, work 3 sts (+ 1 additionally picked up st for hole prevention) for the sleeve, place m (= BoR); in the following round, knit the 2 extra sts together with the adjoining sts as described above (= 50/54/56/58 sts).

At height 3.1 in. (8 cm) from begin of Sleeve, during a knit round, work increases for the first time as follows:

Inc Rnd: K2, M1L, knit to last 2 sts of rnd, M1L, k2 (= 52/56/58/60 sts).

Repeat increases in every 10th rnd 9 times more (= 70/74/76/78 sts).

Continue in garter stitch in the round, working until Sleeve either measures approx. 16.5 in. (42 cm) or is 2 in. (5 cm) shorter than desired length. In the following knit rnd, work the sts as follows: *k1, k2tog, rep from * to end of rnd, ending with "k1/2/1/–."

Change to DPN set size US 7 (4.5 mm), and work in ribbing pattern for 2 in. (5 cm). Bind off all sts using elastic BO method.

FINISHING

Neatly weave in all ends. Turn the garment inside out, gently pin it into shape on an even horizontal surface, cover it with a moistened cloth, and let it dry.

CABLE CHART

pattern repeat = 10 sts

LEGEND

▣	= knit 1
▮	= purl 1
▣▣▣▣ (cable)	= cable 4 sts to the left: hold 2 sts on cable needle in front of work, k2, then knit the sts from the cable needle
▣▣▣▣ (cable)	= cable 4 sts to the right: hold 2 sts on cable needle behind work, k2, then knit the sts from the cable needle

Matching Accessories

SIZES

One size

Height 8.7 in. (22 cm)

MATERIALS

◆ ggh Norvika; #5 bulky weight; 30% Norwegian
   wool, 30% acrylic, 20% alpaca, 13% bio-polyamide:
   Biofeel®, 7% polyamide; 70 yd. (65 m) per 1.75 oz.
   (50 g); 2 skeins #05 Dunkelblau (Dark Blue)

◆ DPN sets in sizes US 6 (4.0 mm) and US 7 (4.5
   mm)

◆ tapestry needle for weaving in ends

GAUGE

In ribbing pattern on US 7 (4.5 mm) needles: 16 sts and
20 rows/rounds = 4 x 4 in. (10 x 10 cm)

STITCH PATTERNS

Ribbing pattern in the round

Alternate "k2, p2" to end of round.

INSTRUCTIONS

Using DPN set in size US 6 (4.0 mm), CO 76 sts. Join in
the round, placing a marker for the BoR. Work 8 rnds in
ribbing pattern.

Change to DPN set in size US 7 (4.5 mm) and continue
in ribbing pattern.

At 8.3 in. (21 cm) height from CO row, begin crown
decreases as follows:

Rnd 1 (dec rnd): *K2tog, p2, rep from * to end of rnd
(= 57 sts).

Rnd 2 (dec rnd): *K1, p2tog, rep from * to end of rnd
(= 38 sts).

Rnd 3 (dec rnd): *K1, p1, k1, k2tog, p1, rep from * to end
of rnd, ending with k1, p1 (= 32 sts).

Rnd 4: Work all sts as they appear (knit the knits and
purl the purls).

Using working yarn held double, run a needle through
remaining stitches and cinch to close the small opening.

FINISHING

Weave in all ends.

ARNA
Leg warmers

◆◆◆

SIZES

One size

Height 11.8 in. (30 cm)

MATERIALS

◆ Hey Mama Wolf Schafwolle No. 03; #4 medium weight; 100% organic wool; 284 yd. (260 m) per 3.5 oz. (100 g); 1 skein each Krapp (Crimson) and Seabird

◆ DPN sets in sizes US 2.5 (3.0 mm) and US 6 (4.0 mm)

◆ tapestry needle for weaving in ends

◆ stitch markers

GAUGE

In stranded colorwork pattern with two colors on US 6 (4.0 mm) needles: 19 sts and 29 rows/rounds = 4 x 4 in. (10 x 10 cm)

COLOR DESIGNATIONS

MC: Crimson

CC: Seabird

STITCH PATTERNS

Ribbing pattern in the round

Alternate "k2, p2" to end of round.

Stockinette stitch in the round

Knit all stitches in all rounds.

Stranded colorwork pattern in the round

Work all rnds in st st according to the colorwork chart. Repeat the pattern repeat [18 sts wide] throughout the round. Work Rnds 1–41 once.

PLEASE NOTE: Lock in floats after every 3rd stitch.

INSTRUCTIONS

Using DPN set in size US 2.5 (3.0 mm) and MC, CO 52 sts. Join in the round, placing a marker for the BoR. Work 12 rnds in ribbing pattern.

Change to DPN set in size US 6 (4.0 mm).

Knit 1 rnd, increasing 2 sts evenly distributed (= 54 sts).

Work stranded colorwork pattern from colorwork chart. Repeat the pattern repeat [18 sts wide] throughout the round. Work Rnds 1–41 once.

Knit 1 rnd, decreasing 2 sts evenly distributed (= 52 sts).

Change to DPN set in size US 2.5 (3.0 mm), and work 12 rnds in ribbing pattern.

Bind off all sts using elastic BO method.

FINISHING

Weave in all ends.

LEGEND

 = MC: Crimson

= CC: Seabird

= M1L

COLORWORK CHART

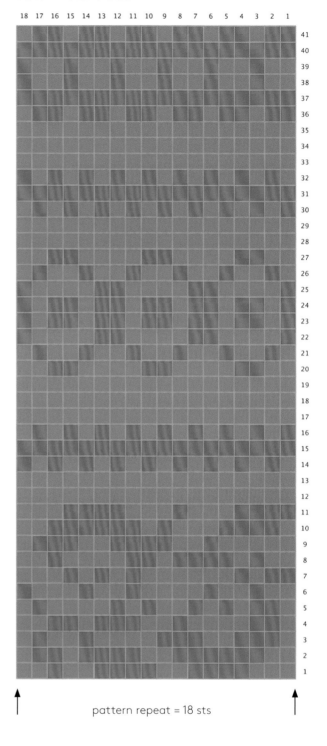

pattern repeat = 18 sts

ÁSDÍS Hat

SIZES

One size

Height 8.3 in. (21 cm)

MATERIALS

- Lana Grossa Alta Moda Alpaca; #4 medium weight; 90% alpaca, 5% pure new wool, 5% polyamide; 153 yd. (140 m) per 1.75 oz. (50 g); 2 skeins #15 Grau/Beige Meliert (Gray/Beige Heathered) and 1 skein #14 Rohweiß (Natural White)
- circular needle size US 4 (3.5 mm), 16 in. (40 cm) long
- circular needle size US 6 (4.0 mm), 16 in. (40 cm) long
- tapestry needle for weaving in ends
- stitch markers(s)
- pom-pom maker, 2.4 in. (6 cm)

GAUGE

Stockinette stitch on US 6 (4.0 mm) needles: 26 sts and 30 rows/rounds = 4 x 4 in. (10 x 10 cm)

COLOR DESIGNATIONS

MC: Gray/Beige Heathered

CC: Natural White

STITCH PATTERNS

Ribbing pattern in the round

Alternate "k2, p2" to end of round.

Stockinette stitch in the round

Knit all stitches in all rounds.

INSTRUCTIONS

With size US 4 (3.5 mm) circular needle, in MC, CO 104 sts. Join in the round, placing a marker for the BoR. Work 14 rnds in ribbing pattern.

Change to needle size US 6 (4.0 mm), and work st st.

At 7.9 in. (20 cm) overall height from CO edge, begin crown decreases as follows:

Dec Rnd 1: *K8, skp, rep from * to end of rnd, ending with k4 (= 94 sts).

Work 1 rnd even without decreases in st st.

Dec Rnd 2: K8, skp, *k7, skp, rep from * to end of rnd, ending with k3 (= 84 sts).

Work 1 rnd even without decreases in st st.

Dec Rnd 3: K8, skp, *k6, skp, rep from *, ending with k2 (= 74 sts).

Dec Rnd 4: K8, skp, *k4, skp, rep from * (=54 sts).

Work 1 more rnd even without decreases in st st.

Using working yarn held double, run a needle through remaining stitches and cinch to close.

FINISHING

Weave in ends. Make a pom-pom in CC, and sew it to the top of the hat.

DAGUR
Hat

◆◆◆

SIZES

One size

Height 8 in. (20 cm)

MATERIALS

- Rauwerk Merino Sportweight; #2 fine weight; 100% merino wool; 328 yd. (300 m) per 3.5 oz. (100 g); 1 skein Graphit (Gray) and small amounts of Obsidian (Dark Gray) and Quarz (Light Gray)
- DPN sets in sizes US 2.5 (3.0 mm), US 4 (3.5 mm), and US 6 (4.0 mm)
- tapestry needle for weaving in ends
- stitch markers

GAUGE

Stockinette stitch in one color on US 4 (3.5 mm) needles: 19 sts and 30 rows/rounds = 4 x 4 in. (10 x 10 cm)

PLEASE NOTE: Since everybody knits differently, the stranded colorwork pattern should be swatched to determine whether a smaller or larger needle size might be required to match the listed gauge. Needle size US 6 (4.0 mm) is recommended.

COLOR DESIGNATIONS

MC: Gray

CC1: Dark Gray

CC2: Light Gray

STITCH PATTERNS

Ribbing pattern in the round

Alternate "k2, p2" to end of round.

Stockinette stitch in the round

Knit all stitches in all rounds.

Stranded colorwork pattern in the round

Work all rnds in st st according to the colorwork chart. Repeat the pattern repeat [7 sts wide] throughout the round. Work Rnds 1–17 once.

PLEASE NOTE: Lock in floats after every 3rd stitch. Keep CC at the base of the finger, i.e., in front.

INSTRUCTIONS

Using DPN set in size US 2.5 (3.0 mm) and CC1, CO 112 sts. Join in the round, placing a marker for the BoR, then work in ribbing pattern for 2 in. (5 cm).

Change to DPN set size US 6 (4.0 mm), and continue, working in stranded colorwork pattern according to Colorwork Chart.

Repeat the pattern repeat [7 sts wide] 16 times per round. Work Rnds 1–17 once.

Now, change to MC and needle size US 4 (3.5 mm), and begin crown decreases as follows:

Dec Rnd 1: *K1, k2tog, k1, rep from * to end of rnd (= 84 sts).

Work 4 rnds even without decreases in st st.

Dec Rnd 2: *K1, k2tog twice, k1, rep from * to end of rnd (= 56 sts).

Work 6 rnds even without decreases in st st.

Dec Rnd 3: *K1, k2tog, k1, rep from * to end of rnd (= 42 sts).

Work 4 rnds even without decreases in st st.

Dec Rnd 4: *K1, k2tog, rep from * to end of rnd (= 28 sts).

Work 1 rnd even without decreases in st st.

Using working yarn held double, run a needle through the remaining sts and cinch to close.

COLORWORK CHART

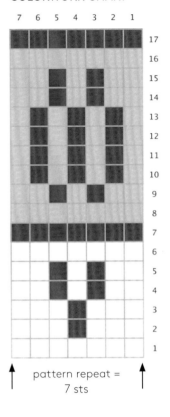

pattern repeat = 7 sts

LEGEND

= MC: Gray

= CC1: Dark Gray

= CC2: Light Gray

GUDBJÖRG
Cowl

◆◆◆

SIZE

Circumference 26 in. (66 cm), height 9.8 in. (25 cm)

MATERIALS

- ◆ Lana Grossa Bingo; #4 medium weight; 100% pure new wool; 88 yd. (80 m) per 1.75 oz. (50 g); 3 skeins #24 Schwarz (Black) and 1 skein each #726 Purpurrot (Crimson Red), #728 Kiwigrün (Kiwi Green), and #727 Blaupetrol (Blue Petrol)
- ◆ circular needle size US 6 (4.0 mm), 16 in. (40 cm) long
- ◆ tapestry needle for weaving in ends
- ◆ stitch markers

GAUGE

In Brioche on US 6 (4.0 mm) needles: 15 sts and 22 rows/rounds = 4 x 4 in. (10 x 10 cm)

COLOR DESIGNATIONS

MC: Black

CC1: Crimson Red

CC2: Kiwi Green

CC3: Blue Petrol

STITCH PATTERNS

Two-color Brioche in the round

Setup Rnd (MC): *K1, slip 1 st purlwise together with a yarn over (= sl1-pw+yo), rep from * to end of rnd.

Rnd 1 (CC): *Sl1-pw+yo, purl the slipped st together with the yo of the previous rnd, rep from * to end of rnd.

Rnd 2 (MC): *Knit the slipped st together with the yo of the previous rnd, sl1-pw+yo, rep from * to end of rnd.

Repeat Rnds 1 and 2 for pattern.

INSTRUCTIONS

Using circular needle size US 6 (4.0 mm) and MC, CO 98 sts. Join in the round, placing a marker for the BoR. In MC, work Setup Rnd once, then work two-color Brioche: First, work 4.7 in. (12 cm) in MC and CC1, then 3.1 in. (8 cm) in MC and CC2, and finally, 2 in. (5 cm) in MC and CC3.

At 10 in. (25 cm) overall height, BO all sts using MC and elastic BO method, always working 1 st in pattern, then passing the previous st over st just worked.

FINISHING

Weave in all ends.

HULDA AND HAFDÍS
Hat and mittens

◆◆◇

SIZES

Hat

One size

Height 8.7 in. (22 cm)

Mittens

Width 3.75 in. (9.5 cm)

MATERIALS

- Schachenmayr Cosy Wool; #4 medium weight; 64% rayon/viscose, 25% acrylic, 11% wool; 109 yd. (100 m) per 1.75 oz. (50 g); 2 skeins each #52 Cloud and #22 Gold
- DPN sets size US 6 (4.0 mm), US 7 (4.5 mm), and US 8 (5.0 mm)
- cable needle or auxiliary needle
- safety pin
- tapestry needle for weaving in ends
- stitch markers(s)
- pom-pom maker, 2.4 in. (6 cm)

GAUGE

Garter stitch with cable pattern on US 8 (5.0 mm) needles: 19 sts and 30 rows/rounds = 4 x 4 in. (10 x 10 cm)

COLOR DESIGNATIONS

MC: Cloud

CC: Gold

STITCH PATTERNS

Ribbing pattern in the round

Alternate "k2, p2" to end of round.

Garter stitch in the round

Rnd 1: Knit all sts (= knit rnd).

Rnd 2: Purl all sts (= purl rnd).

Repeat Rounds 1 and 2 throughout.

Cable pattern

In all rounds, work from Cable Chart. Repeat the pattern repeat [8 sts wide] widthwise and Rnds 1–16 heightwise.

INSTRUCTIONS

HAT

Using DPN set size US 6 (4.0 mm) and MC, CO 80 sts. Join in the round, placing a marker for the BoR. Work 12 rnds in ribbing pattern.

Change to DPN set in size US 8 (5.0 mm) and work Cable pattern from chart. Work the pattern repeat [8 sts wide] 8 times per round. Work Rnds 1–16 until an overall height of 7.5 in. (19 cm) from cast-on has been reached. Now, work crown decreases as follows:

Rnd 1 (dec rnd): *K2tog, p2, rep from * to end of rnd (= 60 sts).

Rnd 2 (dec rnd): *K1, p2tog, rep from * to end of rnd (= 40 sts).

Rnd 3 (dec rnd): *K1, p1, k1, k2tog, p1, rep from * to end of rnd, ending with "k1, p1" (= 36 sts)

Rnd 4: Work all sts as they appear (knit the knits and purl the purls).

Using working yarn held double, run needle through remaining sts and cinch to close.

FINISHING

Weave in ends. Make a pom-pom in CC, and sew it to the top of the hat.

MITTENS

On the right mitten, the palm side of the mitten is worked over the sts of needles 1 and 2, and the back of the hand over the sts of needles 3 and 4.

On the left mitten, the palm side of the mitten is worked over the sts of needles 3 and 4, and the back of the hand over the sts of needles 1 and 2.

For the thumb, a thumb opening is worked, to which the thumb is added later.

RIGHT MITTEN

Using DPN set in size US 6 (4.0 mm) and CC, CO 28 sts and distribute evenly onto 4 DPNs (= 7 sts per needle). Join in the round. Place a marker for the BoR.

Work in ribbing pattern for 30 rnds (= 4.7 in [12 cm]).

Change to DPN set in size US 7 (4.5 mm). Work the sts of needle 1, those of needle 2, as well as the first 2 sts of needle 3 in garter stitch. Work the Cable pattern over 10 sts of needles 3 and 4. Work the next-to-last and last st of needle 4 in garter stitch.

At height of 2.8 in. (7 cm) from cuff, work the thumb opening on needle 1. For this, work 1 st, and transfer the remaining 6 sts to a safety pin for holding. CO 6 new sts onto needle 1, and finish the round in pattern. Continue to work in pattern.

At an overall height of 5.9 in. (15 cm) from cuff, after a pattern round with cable crossing, work a total of 10 rnds of tip decreases. For this, work all sts in garter stitch in the round, decreasing in every purl rnd a total of 5 times as follows:

Needles 1 + 3: P1, p2tog, p to end of this needle.

Needles 2 + 4: P to last 3 sts on this needle, p2tog, p1.

Thread working yarn held double through the remaining 8 sts, and cinch to close the opening at the tip.

For the thumb, place the formerly held 6 thumb sts from the safety pin onto needle 1 of a size US 7 (4.5 mm) DPN set and, using needles 2 and 3, pick up and knit 4 additional sts each from the additionally CO sts at the thumb (= 14 sts). Work 1 rnd in garter stitch.

Continue in garter stitch, and in the following round, on needles 2 and 3, knit together the thumb sts as follows:

Needle 1: Work all sts in pattern.

Needle 2: Knit the first stitch together with the second stitch in pattern.

Needle 3: Knit the next-to-last stitch together with the last stitch in pattern (= 12 sts = 4 sts per needle).

Now, continue in garter stitch. At an overall height of 2.4 in. (6 cm), begin tip decreases, working 4 rnds while decreasing 2 times in a purl rnd as follows:

Needle 1: P2tog (first and second sts); work to last 2 sts of this needle, p2tog (last 2 sts).

Needle 2: P2tog (first stitch with the second stitch).

Needle 3: P2tog (last 2 sts).

Thread working yarn held double through the remaining 4 sts, and cinch to close the opening.

LEFT MITTEN

Work as the right mitten, but work the palm section over the sts of needles 3 and 4, and the back of the hand over the sts of needles 1 and 2.

FINISHING

Weave in ends.

CABLE PATTERN CHART

	16
	15
	14
	13
	12
	11
	10
	9
	8
	7
	6
	5
	4
	3
	2
	1

pattern repeat = 10 sts

LEGEND

▣ = knit 1

▮ = purl 1

= cable 4 sts to the left: hold 2 sts on cable needle in front of work, k2, then knit the sts from the cable needle

= cable 4 sts to the right: hold 2 sts on cable needle behind work, k2, then knit the sts from the cable needle

DRÍFA
Triangular shawl

SIZE

Long side approx. 79 in. (200 cm), from point to middle of long side approx. 31.5 in. (80 cm)

MATERIALS

- Isager Silk Mohair; #0 lace weight; 75% super kid mohair, 25% silk; 232 yd. (212 m) per 0.9 oz. (25 g); 2 skeins #7 Braun (Brown)

PLEASE NOTE: Check the ball bands, and only use skeins of the same dye lot together. Actual total yardage may vary, depending on individual knitting style.

- circular needle size US 10 (6.0 mm), 32 in. (80 cm) long
- tapestry needle for weaving in ends
- stitch markers

GAUGE

Garter stitch on US 10 (6.0 mm) needles: 12 sts and 24 rows/rounds = 4 x 4 in. (10 x 10 cm)

STITCH PATTERNS

Garter stitch in rows

Knit all stitches in all rows.

Selvedge stitches

Knotted selvedge: *At the beginning of the row, slip the selv st knitwise with yarn in back of work. Now, work the row in pattern to the last st, and knit the selv st at the end of the row. Turn work, and rep from *.

INSTRUCTIONS

The shawl is worked in back-and-forth rows, beginning at the point.

Using size US 10 (6.0 mm) needles, CO 3 sts and work as follows:

Setup Row (WS): Selv st, p1, selv st (= 3 sts).

RS Row: Selv st, M1R, k1 (= ctr st), M1L, selv st (= 2 sts increased).

WS Row: Selv st, k to ctr st, p1, k to last st, selv st.

Repeat these two rows, always knitting the ctr st in RS rows and purling it in WS rows. Increase as stated in every RS row before and after the ctr st. Work all other sts in garter st, and the selv sts as Knotted selvedge.

At an overall height of approx. 31.5 in. (80 cm) (= 120 rows) and overall width of approx. 79 in. (200 cm) (= 245 sts), bind off all sts.

FINISHING

To block, pin the shawl into shape on an even horizontal surface, cover it with a moistened cloth, and let it dry. Weave in ends.

SIF
Beret

♦♦♦

SIZE

One size

Diameter 10.6 in. (27 cm)

MATERIALS

- Isager Alpaca 2; #1 super fine weight; 50% alpaca, 50% wool; 273 yd. (250 m) per 1.75 oz. (50 g); 1 skein each #Eco-7s Braun (Brown) and #59 Gold
- DPN sets in sizes US 7 (4.5 mm) and US 8 (5.0 mm)
- circular needle size US 8 (5.0 mm), 16 in. (40 cm) long
- circular needle size US 7 (4.5 mm), 16 in. (40 cm) long
- circular needle size US 6 (4.0 mm), 16 in. (40 cm) long
- tapestry needle for weaving in ends
- 16 stitch markers

GAUGE

Stockinette stitch with yarn held double on US 7 (4.5 mm) needles: 20 sts and 22 rows/rounds = 4 x 4 in. (10 x 10 cm)

COLOR DESIGNATIONS

MC: Brown

CC: Gold

PLEASE NOTE: MC and CC are worked with yarn held double throughout.

STITCH PATTERNS

Two-color ribbing pattern in the round

Alternate "k1 in MC, k2 in CC" to end of round.

Stockinette stitch in the round

Knit all stitches in all rounds.

Stranded colorwork pattern in the round

Work all rnds in st st, following the appropriate chart. Repeat the pattern repeat [initially 2 sts wide] width-wise. Work Rnds 1–27 once, increasing in every other round as shown.

PLEASE NOTE: Lock in floats after every other stitch.

INSTRUCTIONS

Beret is knit from the top down. With 2 strands of MC held together and 2 DPNs from a US 7 (4.5 mm) DPN set, CO 4 sts, and work a short i-cord as follows: *k4, do not turn work, but slide the 4 sts to the other end of the needle. Lead the working yarn in back of work to the beginning of the needle once more, and again k4, rep from * twice.

In the next row, increase as follows:

Inc Rnd: *K1, M1L, rep from * 3 times (= 8 sts).

Distribute the 8 sts onto 4 DPNs. Join in the round, placing a marker for the BoR.

Using DPN set in size US 8 (5.0 mm), work the stranded colorwork pattern according to the colorwork chart. Repeat the pattern repeat [initially 2 sts wide] throughout the round. Work Rnds 1–27 once, increasing in every other rnd as shown (= 112 sts). For better orientation, place markers between pattern repeats. If needed, change to US 8 (5.0 mm) circular needle. During the last rnd of the stranded pattern, place markers in every pattern repeat, always before and after the first and fifteenth stitches (= 16 markers total), and carry these markers up in the following increase rnds. When encountering these markers in the following rnds, increase before and after each m, and knit the st beween the markers. Change to circular needle size US 7 (4.5 mm). Work in MC in st st, increasing as follows:

Rnd 1: Knit all sts.

Rnd 2 (inc rnd): Knit, working M1R before the st enclosed in markers, and M1L after it (= 16 sts increased = 128 sts).

Rnds 3–5: Knit all sts.

Rnd 6 (inc rnd): Knit to 1 st before the st enclosed in markers, then M1R, k1, M1L, knit the st enclosed in markers, M1R, k1, M1L; knit to next marker and repeat around (= 32 sts increased = 160 sts).

Rnd 7: Knit all sts.

Rnd 8 (inc rnd): Knit to 3 sts before the st enclosed in markers, then M1R, k3, k the st enclosed in markers, k3, M1L (= 16 sts increased = 176 sts).

Work 4 rnds in st st.

Now, continue in st st, decreasing as follows:

Rnd 1: Knit all sts.

Rnd 2 (dec rnd): Knit each st enclosed in markers together with the following st; place markers on either side of this st (= 8 sts decreased = 168 sts).

Rnd 3: Knit all sts.

Rnd 4 (dec rnd): Slip the sts enclosed in markers knitwise, k2tog the next 2 sts, then pass the slipped st over, mark the resulting st again with 2 markers, one before and another one after this stitch (= 16 sts decreased = 152 sts).

Rnd 5: Knit all sts.

Rnd 6: Repeat Rnd 4 (= 136 sts).

Rnd 7: Knit all sts.

Rnd 8 (dec rnd): Knit each st enclosed in markers together with the following st; place markers on either side of this st (= 8 sts decreased = 128 sts).

Rnd 9: Knit all sts.

Repeat Rnds 8 and 9 twice (= 112 sts).

Now, change to circular needle size US 7 (4.5 mm) and work 6 rnds in ribbing pattern. Tightly BO all sts in CC.

FINISHING

Weave in all ends. Pin the beret into shape, cover it with a moistened cloth, and let it dry.

COLORWORK CHART

	28	27	26	25	24	23	22	21	20	19	18	17	16	15	14	13	12	11	10	9	8	7	6	5	4	3	2	1	

27

26

25

24

23

22

21

20

19

18

17

16

15

14

13

12

11

10

9

8

7

6

5

4

3

2

1

pattern repeat at begin = 2 sts

LEGEND

 = MC: Brown

 = CC: Gold

 = M1R

= M1L

KOLBRÚN
Headband

SIZE

One size

Width 4 in. (10 cm), circumference 20.5 in. (52 cm) (unstretched)

MATERIALS

- Isager Alpaca 2; #1 super fine weight; 50% alpaca, 50% wool; 273 yd. (250 m) per 1.75 oz. (50 g); 1 skein #21 Rot (Red)
- circular needle size US 6 (4.0 mm), 16 in. (40 cm) long
- cable needle or auxiliary needle
- tapestry needle for weaving in ends
- stitch markers

GAUGE

In Cable pattern with yarn held double on US 6 (4.0 mm): 30 sts and 26 rows/rounds = 4 x 4 in. (10 x 10 cm)

STITCH PATTERNS

Cable pattern worked over 28 sts widthwise

Work from Cable Chart. Only RS (odd-numbered) rows are shown; in WS (even-numbered) rows, knit the knits and purl the purls. Work the pattern [pattern repeat 28 sts wide] as stated in the instructions. Repeat Rnds 1–16 for pattern.

Selvedge stitches

Knotted selvedge: *At the beginning of the row, slip the selv st knitwise with yarn in back of work. Then, work the row in pattern to the last st, and knit the selv st at the end of the row. Turn work, and rep from *.

PLEASE NOTE: The yarn is held double throughout.

INSTRUCTIONS

Using circular needle size US 6 (4.0 mm) and yarn held double, CO 30 sts. Between the selv sts of the knotted selvedge, work Cable pattern over 28 sts. Repeat Rnds 1–16 to a height of 21.3 in. (54 cm), ending with a WS row in purl. BO all sts in the following RS row using elastic BO method.

FINISHING

Sew the short edges of the band together from the RS in mattress stitch, closing it into a ring shape. Neatly weave in all ends.

LEGEND

▣	= knit 1
▮	= purl 1
▣◹▣	= cable 2 sts to the left: hold 1 st on cable needle in front of work, k1, then knit the st from the cable needle
▣◸▣	= cable 2 sts to the right: hold 1 st on cable needle in back of work, k1, then knit the st from the cable needle
▣▣◸▣▣	= cable 4 sts to the right: hold 2 sts on cable needle in back of work, k2, then knit the sts from the cable needle
▣▣◹▣▣	= cable 4 sts to the left: hold 2 sts on cable needle in front of work, k2, then knit the sts from the cable needle

CABLE CHART

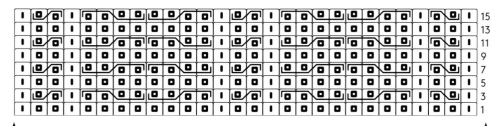

pattern repeat = 28 sts

SNORRI
Socks

◆◆◇

SIZES

W5½/6, W7/8, W9/9½–M7/7½, W11/12–M8½/9, M10/11]

Total length including heel and toe: approx. 8.9/9.5/10/10.4/10.8 in. (22.5/24/25.5/26.5/27.5 cm)

PLEASE NOTE: Numbers for individual sizes are listed in order from smallest to largest size, divided by slashes. If only one number is given, it applies to all sizes.

PLEASE NOTE: Since this yarn is very stretchy, the socks can be worked slightly shorter than usual.

MATERIALS

◆ Lana Grossa McWool; #2 fine weight; 50% cotton, 50% acrylic; 109 yd. (100 m) per 1.75 oz. (50 g); 3 skeins #120 Schwarz (Black) and 1 skein #114 Petrol

PLEASE NOTE: Check the ball bands, and only use skeins of the same dye lot together. Actual total yardage may vary, depending on individual knitting style.

◆ DPN sets in sizes US 4 (3.5 mm) and US 5 (4.0 mm)

◆ tapestry needle for weaving in ends

◆ stitch markers

◆ stitch holder or waste yarn

GAUGE

Stockinette stitch in one color on US 6 (4.0 mm): 21 sts and 25 rows/rounds = 4 x 4 in. (10 x 10 cm)

COLOR DESIGNATIONS

MC: Black

CC: Petrol

STITCH PATTERNS

Ribbing pattern in the round

Alternate "k2, p2" to end of round.

Stockinette stitch in the round

Knit all stitches in all rounds.

Stranded colorwork pattern in the round

Work all rnds in st st according to the colorwork chart. Repeat the pattern repeat [8 sts wide] throughout the round. Work Rnds 1–22 as often as stated in the instructions.

Stockinette stitch in back-and-forth rows

In RS rows, knit all sts; in WS rows, purl all sts.

INSTRUCTIONS

Using DPN set in size US 4 (3.5 mm) and MC, CO 32/32/40/40/48 sts, and distribute the sts evenly between the needles. Join in the round, placing a marker for the BoR. For the cuff, work 2 in. (5 cm) in ribbing pattern, then change to DPN set size US 6 (4.0 mm).

Now, work the stranded colorwork pattern from the colorwork chart, working the pattern repeat [8 sts wide] 4/4/5/5/6 times widthwise per round. Work Rnds 1–22 twice heightwise.

At overall height of 8.3 in. (21 cm), begin working a boomerang heel in CC (see page 20).

For the heel, divide sts as follows for your size: 5–6–5/5–6–5/7–6–7/7–6–7/8–8–8 sts.

After the heel has been finished, continue working over all sts in stranded colorwork pattern according to the colorwork chart.

For size W5½/6: Work Rnds 1–22 once, then work only Rnds 1–14 once.

For size W7/8: Work Rnds 1–22 once, then work only Rnds 1–21 once.

For size W9/9½–M7/7½: Work Rnds 1–22 twice.

For size W11/12–M8½/9: Work Rnds 1–22 twice, then work only Rnds 1–2 once.

For size M10/11: Work Rnds 1–22 twice, then work only Rnds 1–4 once.

At length of approx. 7.3/7.9/8.3/8.7/9 in. (18.5/20/21/22/23 cm) (including the heel), begin working toe decreases in MC in st st (see page 21).

FINISHING

Weave in all ends neatly.

COLORWORK CHART

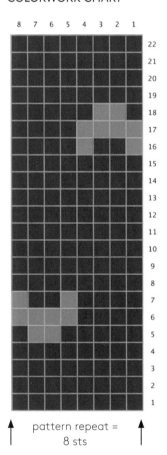

pattern repeat =
8 sts

LEGEND

= MC: Black

= CC: Petrol

ABOUT THE AUTHOR

Wenke Müller has been developing hand knitting patterns under her brand name tomkeknits since 2017. Her style, timeless and contemporary at the same time, is streamlined and yet designed with attention to detail and a love for more unusual techniques.

Holding a degree in fashion design, she had worked for the theater and in various design studios, and she created high-end knitwear for the international fashion industry before returning to hand knitting—a passion that started in childhood—while staying at home with her two children.

In addition to *Top-Down Colorwork Knit Sweaters and Accessories*, she has published two books in German with Edition Michael Fischer, *Hygge Babys & Kids* and *Hygge Accessories*.

Today, Wenke Müller lives with her family in her hometown of Dresden. Under the brand name tomkeknits, she creates her own designs as well as knitwear for various yarn manufacturers and magazines.

You can follow her Instagram handle **@tomkeknits** and show off your own projects made from her patterns using hashtag #tomkeknits.

https://tomkeknits.com

www.ravelry.com/designers/wenke-muller

ACKNOWLEDGMENTS

When asked in the spring of 2019 by my editor, Anja Sommerfeld, whether I would like to write a book of beautiful colorwork pullovers, just half a year had passed since my second book, *Hygge Accessories*, had been published. Accordingly, I was somewhat hesitant in regard to the expected workload, but also very, very excited and curious what designs I would come up with on this topic! I was looking especially forward to the wonderful abundance of yarn choices with which I would have the opportunity to work again.

And, yes, I got down to business right away. During many a weekend and evening, I studied the logistics and construction of top-down circular yoke sweaters featuring stranded colorwork—much obliged to my two lovely children, who had to make do without motherly attention many a time! In exchange for this deprivation, we got, in my opinion, a truly beautiful book with stunning garments for men and women, including classic stranded colorwork patterns as well as solid-colored designs. I'm sure it contains many a treasure to discover for every knitter. Thank you, Anja, for your call!

A very big Thank You goes to my test and sample knitters: Andrea Goverts, Ulrike Ackermann, Sarah Hasenauer, Marion Reinfels, and my mom, Ute Müller.

Furthermore, I would like to express my gratitude to the following yarn sponsors: Hey Mama Wolf, Isager, Rauwerk, ggh, Lana Grossa, Rowan, and Schachenmayr.

And, last but not least, I would like to also express my heartfelt thanks to my dear technical editor, Regina Sidabras, with whom I had the opportunity to cooperate for the third time now, which has been a great pleasure, as always.